ITINERARIES

OTHER BOOKS BY
PHILIP RESNICK

— NON-FICTION —

The Land of Cain (1977)

Parliament vs. People (1984)

Letters to a Québécois Friend (1990)

The Masks of Proteus (1990)

Toward a Canada-Quebec Union (1991)

Thinking English Canada (1994)

Twenty-First Century Democracy (1997)

The Politics of Resentment (2000)

The European Roots of Canadian Identity (2005)

The Labyrinth of North American Identities (2012)

— POETRY —

Between Two Holocausts (1962)

Poems for Andromache (1975)

Poems of Pelion (1979)

The Centaur's Mountain (1986)

Footsteps of the Past (2015)

Passageways (2018)

ITINERARIES

An Intellectual Odyssey

PHILIP RESNICK

RONSDALE PRESS

RONSDALE PRESS
3350 West 21st Avenue, Vancouver, B.C. Canada V6S 1G7
www.ronsdalepress.com

Typesetting: Julie Cochrane, in Caslon 11.5 pt on 15
Cover Design: Julie Cochrane
Paper: Ancient Forest Friendly Enviro 100 edition, 70 lb. Husky (FSC),
    100% post-consumer waste, totally chlorine-free and acid-free.

Ronsdale Press wishes to thank the following for their support of its publishing program: the Canada Council for the Arts, the Government of Canada, the British Columbia Arts Council, and the Province of British Columbia through the British Columbia Book Publishing Tax Credit program.

Library and Archives Canada Cataloguing in Publication

Title: Itineraries: an intellectual odyssey / Philip Resnick.

Names: Resnick, Philip, author.

Description: Includes bibliographical references.

Identifiers: Canadiana (print) 20200157809 | Canadiana (ebook) 20200157817 | ISBN 9781553806028 (softcover) | ISBN 9781553806035 (HTML) | ISBN 9781553806042 (PDF)

Subjects: LCSH: Resnick, Philip. | LCSH: Political scientists — Canada — Biography. | LCSH: Political science teachers — Canada — Biography. | LCSH: University of British Columbia — Faculty — Biography. | LCSH: Canada — Politics and government. | LCSH: National characteristics, Canadian. | CSH: Poets, Canadian (English)—Biography | LCGFT: Autobiographies.

Classification: LCC JC253.R47 A3 2020 | DDC 320.092—dc23

At Ronsdale Press we are committed to protecting the environment. To this end we are working with Canopy and printers to phase out our use of paper produced from ancient forests. This book is one step towards that goal.

Printed in Canada by Island Blue, Victoria, B.C.

*for Theo and Gabe, whose generation will
inherit what my generation and that of
our children will bequeath them*

ACKNOWLEDGEMENTS

My thanks to a number of friends who read an
earlier version of this manuscript and provided helpful comments:
Mark Abley, Duncan Cameron, Frank Cunningham, and John
Richards. A special thanks is due to my late colleague,
Alan Cairns, who first suggested to me — somewhat to my
disbelief — that I should think of writing a memoir.
Lastly, I would like to acknowledge Ron Hatch, who has
pushed and prodded me to make this a better manuscript
than it might otherwise have been.

CONTENTS

THE RIVER OF YOUR CHILDHOOD

You would return to the river of your childhood,
to the faces old and young,
to the streetcars and the bustle
and the dreams you half pursued,
careless adolescent playing hopscotch with your youth.
Did you know where the journey might lead you,
the outer goal posts,
the chance encounters,
the fermented passions that turn into despair?
Can't you see them in the mirror,
the creases and the wrinkles,
the atrophying muscles,
can't you hear the catalogue
aged sufferers in distress recite to one another
like catechisms from a vanished faith?
"Hold on," you want to say,
"Surely you can muster a cheer or two
for the promises, small but tangible,
you did fulfill,
for the friends you acquired,
the bits of wisdom which came your way."
The river of your childhood runs outward
and where it mingles
with a hundred other rivers
has become home to your *imaginaire*.

CHAPTER 1

The Third Solitude

THE MONTREAL INTO which I was born towards the end of World War II consisted of three solitudes — the French, the English, and a number of ethnic communities, in my case the Jewish. Each of these communities was a world onto itself, and I will set off on this venture with a description of what that has meant for me.

The first language I heard, the one spoken by my parents, was Yiddish. My parents had immigrated to Canada in the years just before the full onslaught of the Great Depression, my father from Belarus, my mother from Poland. My father had a set of brothers and a sister, most of them in the United States, one back in the Soviet Union. My mother's family, with the exception of the brother who had sponsored her immigration, were wiped out in the horror of the Final Solution.

I grew up with Yiddish in my immediate background, but with English the language of communication with my two older siblings and with the children who would become my classmates and friends in the parochial Jewish school to which I would eventually be sent. This was very much the pattern for Jewish immigrants of East European background and their offspring in Montreal — linguistic assimilation into the English-speaking community, rather than the French, coupled with the maintenance of strong communal and religious institutions of their own.

My mother, more so than my father, was strongly Orthodox in her faith, so Friday-night candles, Sabbath and holiday observance, and a kosher home were *de rigueur*. Attending an elementary school and subsequently for three years a high school where the teaching of Hebrew, biblical subjects, and related Jewish themes were part of the curriculum, would only reinforce this. Until the age of fifteen or sixteen, I had little reason to question the world into which I had been born.

If anything, I followed the precepts of my faith with little hesitation, attending synagogue on a regular weekly basis once I had come of age, going through the ritual of a Bar Mitzvah, identifying strongly with what was then the newly formed state of Israel and the many trials and tribulations it would have to face. And in the background, never entirely forgotten amidst the snatches of Yiddish and stories of the old country and the music and pictures, was the Holocaust, and the deep fissures it had left.

What led me eventually to take my distance from the faith of my fathers? This is not all that easy to answer from the distance of so many years, but a number of thoughts come to mind. Reading was an important part of my upbringing, beginning with the borrowing of books from the Jewish Public Library, then located on Esplanade and Mount Royal, and strongly reinforced in my adolescent years at Herzliah High School. The world of my reading, whether the *Grimm's Fairy Tales* or the *Hardy Boys* of my childhood, or the more serious *War and Peace* or *Jean-Christophe* of my adolescence broadened my outlook, bringing me into contact with a much larger sphere than the strictly Jewish world of my youth.

Then there was the reality of the cultural and political world all around me. As I grew up, I became more conscious of the two major solitudes which made Montreal what it was: the anglophone world I would enter more definitively in my final high school year at Outremont High and subsequent undergraduate years at McGill; the francophone world I could sense from the bookstores whose windows I would contemplate on Laurier Avenue on a Saturday afternoon and from the early rumblings of what was to become the Quiet Revolution in the aftermath of the death of Maurice Duplessis, Quebec's own little dictator, in September 1959.

Finally, there must have been my temperament, fairly rebellious by nature. I can still remember being the only member of my high school class, at the time of the 1957 federal election, to announce that I would be voting for the Co-operative Commonwealth Federation (CCF), were I to cast a ballot, when most of my fellow students would have been voting Liberal, or in a few cases, Conservative.

I also remember having been part of what must have been one of Canada's very first student rebellions — well before the 1960s — provoked in our case by the firing of a popular principal at Herzliah High School. And I can also remember the first cracks in my faith, as I began to question the "chosen people" passages of the morning and Sabbath prayers — "Why were the Jews more chosen than anyone else?" — leading me in rapid succession to take my distance from the larger religious creed. So it was perhaps no surprise that by Grade 10, in a fit of rebellion, I had thrown the bible on the floor and stamped on it in one of my religious classes at Herzliah High, and had been told in peremptory fashion to remove myself to one of the Protestant Schools (as English-language schools were predominantly known in those years) for my final high school year.

From the age of sixteen on, therefore, I have defined myself as a non-believer. I have had no reason to reconsider my course. But I need to say a few things about my earlier religious upbringing, before delving a little more extensively into the Jewish part of my identity.

To have been religious in one's youth means to understand more clearly just how consoling faith can be to its adherents. Not only can it provide solace for the adversities of everyday and for the fearful mysteries of death, but it also opens the door to a community of the faithful with whom one can share one's beliefs. One's fellow believers can provide assistance, comfort, and a sense of connectedness often lost in the anomic world that surrounds us.

Then there is the metaphysical dimension of religion which seeks to provide an answer to the challenge of cosmic loneliness, which for pre-modern societies, no less than our own, characterizes the human condition. Deities or a deity, be it the nature gods of Indigenous and polytheistic creeds, or the monotheistic version associated with the Abrahamic religions, offer an explanation of sorts for things beyond our comprehension. No wonder agnosticism and atheism were for so long the domain of sceptics and castaways at the margins of mainstream society.

This is less true in our own day and age, at least in the Western world, which has become a good deal less religious in character. And I for one am grateful that I do not have to bear my non-belief as some kind of cross, or be forced to conform to a religious mould against my will, as would have been the norm in an earlier day. But I also understand why many cannot escape the lure of organized religion. I am perfectly happy to live in a pluralist society where religious toleration within a larger secular framework is the norm.

Have I ceased to be a Jew? If one were to define this in a purely religious sense, the answer is clearly Yes. I have only rarely entered a synagogue since abandoning my childhood faith, nor do I feel the slightest desire to return to one. I married a non-Jew, did not raise my two sons with the precepts of organized religion, and have been thoroughly secular in my outlook.

But what about the cultural dimensions of being Jewish? This is another matter, a good deal more complicated than the question of religion. Primo Levi, for example, a thoroughly secular Italian of Jewish background, became conscious of his Jewishness only as a result of his experience in Auschwitz. It did not make him more religious, but it brought home the inescapable character of his background.

I myself and Jews of my generation have been spared such a horrendous experience. Nor have we had to face the systemic anti-Semitism of the blood lands of Eastern Europe, or the more discreet anti-Semitism of the pre-World War II West. We have been free to follow our own stars, making our way as citizens of liberal democratic societies, with exactly the same rights and obligations as everyone else. Happily, persecution is no longer the source of identity for most of us living in the West, as might have been the case earlier.

Yet I cannot deny that at certain moments I do feel intensely Jewish. This was most evident when I finally made it to Central Europe in 1994, visiting the site of the Warsaw Ghetto, Auschwitz and Buchenwald, and contemplating the fate of those who had perished there. It also comes flooding in whenever I have delved into the history of the Jews, found myself walking the byways of Spain's lost Juderías, or revisited the graves of my parents in Montreal.

Something else is involved in my cultural Jewishness that is not encompassed in what I have just described. It is my identification with those who had broken with the old faith or taken some distance from it. Among my Jewish cultural heroes are figures like Baruch Spinoza, excommunicated by the Jewish community of Amsterdam for his heretical views, Heinrich Heine one of the greatest German poets, yet conscious of his Jewish roots, Karl Marx and Rosa Luxemburg, estranged Jews whose revolutionary pedigree needs no underlining. And among others I look up to are figures no more bound by any religious conformism: Einstein and Freud, Kafka and Zweig, Arthur Koestler and Eric Hobsbawm.

Ultimately, it is the prophetic tradition in Judaism with which I can most closely identify. The stern god of the Old Testament is not an appealing figure. He can be authoritarian, patriarchal, heavy-handed, and vindictive in turn — certainly not known for his kindly temper. The prophets speak to a more humanizing side of the religion, one rooted in the historical condition in which ancient Israel/Judea found itself, caught between contending empires and facing destruction at any moment. There is a consoling side to Isaiah, a lamenting one to Jeremiah, a redemptive one to Ezekiel, and a willingness to speak truth to power to Amos which have survived through the millennia. And they have provided the template from which many later figures with a Jewish cultural background have drawn inspiration.

It is a difficult business separating the cultural component of the Jewish tradition from its religious content. One thinks of ethnic foods, e.g. a predilection for bagels or gefilte fish or eggplant dishes, of smart-aleck humour (a defence mechanism when times were tough), of klezmer music with its East European and gypsy over-tones or Ladino music with its evocation of a vanished past. There is a definitive cultural component to Jewish identity in its diasporic setting to which even those with minimal religious belief can relate.

I would emphasize a number of other, pertinent themes: an intellectual predisposition to the written word, an openness to innovative thinking, an ability when necessary to function in multiple tongues, and a deep historical sensitivity to the dangers of persecution and injustice. The biblical and Talmudic tradition placed a great deal of emphasis on literacy among the faithful (at least for males) and this long before the emergence of the printing press or the coming of the Enlightenment.

Frequently expelled from one European country or the other, the Jews were forced to be inventive in order to survive. Having a distinct language for their religious rites forced them to become proficient in the vernacular language of the country within which they dwelt and in some cases in the languages of the countries with which they traded. As an ethnic and religious minority, they often experienced persecution first-hand, making them more sensitive to issues of political or social injustice than many of their non-Jewish counterparts. It is no accident that Jews have been overrepresented historically in movements for reform and revolution.

When I think back on my own intellectual development, I see some of these strands at work. I have already mentioned a predisposition to reading, and this from a fairly early age. I would not overplay how innovative my life has turned out to be, but by my adolescent years I had acquired what the French would call *un esprit de contradiction* and with it a willingness to question and challenge prescribed ideas, no matter their origin.

Having been socialized through Yiddish and to a lesser degree Hebrew from an early age may have made me more open to learning other languages. English was of course a given in the pre-Bill 101 Montreal world in which I grew up. But I would with time come to take French almost as seriously, and would also acquire a smattering of familiarity with languages such as German, Spanish, Russian, and Greek. Finally, I can recall an early inclination to identify with the underdog and to reject the pursuit of money as some kind of end in itself. Did that make me a socialist before my time? Perhaps. More importantly it made me inclined to recognize the importance of combatting social ills and of not subscribing to some long-established status quo simply because it was there.

At times I have been happy to relate to elements of the Jewish cultural tradition. At others, it has been far from my mind. But in writing a memoir of this kind, I must at least acknowledge the role these played in my development.

Where does that leave me when it comes to contemporary Jewish themes, be it the persistence of anti-Semitism in certain quarters, the diversity of the Jewish experience, or the question of Israel and its tangled relations with the Palestinians?

I have been part of the lucky generation, born towards the end or after World War II, and living in a time of general prosperity in North America and the West more generally. I have also been born in one of the world's lucky countries, Canada, far removed from the bloody history of Europe and of the Old World as a whole. So when it comes to anti-Semitism, it has been a less significant part of the political landscape in North America than elsewhere, and less present in the post-war period than might have been true before.

This is not to make light of the existence of a strong current of anti-Semitism in the Canadian past, of the *maudit juif* of a certain French Canadian imagery and of fascist movements like that of Adrien Arcand in the 1930s, of Social Credit in its seminal years in Alberta, of the "None is too many" stance of Frederick Blair, the leading Canadian immigration official, when it came to accepting Jewish refugees fleeing Europe in the 1930s.

In the post-war years, in the aftermath of the Holocaust, and with the increasing focus on human rights, both at the international level through the UN Declaration of 1948, and within Canada, first with the Canadian Bill of Rights of 1960 and subsequently with the Charter of Rights and Freedoms in 1982, the ground has shifted tectonically. For Canadians of Jewish origin of my generation, anti-Semitism has played a much more muted role. This may be less true in Europe, albeit the new current of anti-Semitism one sees in countries like France or Belgium or Germany today has more to do with the rise of Islamism within new migrant communities from the Maghreb, Africa, or the Middle East than with an earlier historical tradition. At the same time, one needs to highlight the role of adherents of the alt-right, both in the United States and in Europe, in perpetuating attacks on synagogues and Jewish community centres and in the defacing of Jewish cemeteries and monuments.

A striking feature of today's Canadian Jewish experience is its great diversity. One sees Chassidic enclaves in cities like Montreal, side by side with mainstream Orthodox, Conservative, Reform, and Reconstructionist congregations. At the same time, rates of intermarriage between Jews and non-Jews across the country are at an all-time high, underlining the degree to which integration into the Canadian mainstream has proceeded apace. Jews have made their mark in all aspects of Canadian life, from politics and the law, to medicine and academic life, to business and the arts. There is no one pathway for Jews to follow and no one voice that can claim to speak for all. As a result, non-believers like myself can claim a Jewish cultural heritage without having to give obeisance to any religious authority or to the official structures of the Jewish community.

This brings me to the question of Israel and its place in the current Jewish *imaginaire*. There can be no gainsaying the historical significance of the creation of a predominantly Jewish state a mere three years after the end of the most horrible catastrophe visited upon the Jewish people in the last 2,000 years. In the cauldron of the concentration camps it mattered little whether one was religious or not, whether one was thoroughly integrated into one's society or lived in a mini-world apart, whether one was Jewish through both parents, one parent, or even a single grandparent. In the road map of the Final Solution, nothing short of the destruction of European Jewry to the last man, woman, or child, would do. In that perverse sense, the Holocaust created a Jewish consciousness even amongst those who had long since cast aside all ties to their religion.

In much the same way, Israel represented a powerful symbol of rebirth, even for the many Jews of the diaspora who had no intention to live there, a country to whose fate they could not be indifferent. All the more since in a number of wars beginning with the one for its independence, Israel seemed to be engaged in an existentialist battle for survival.

The situation, however, has changed dramatically since 1967, with Israel's extension of its control to the whole of pre-1948 Palestine, including the West Bank and, for four decades, Gaza. Suddenly the victims of yesterday found themselves in the driver's seat and the Palestinians appeared as the victims of the piece, without a state of their own. Successive peace efforts and UN resolutions have failed to resolve the conflict. And increasingly, through settlements in the former West Bank, Israel has encroached on what should have been the basis for a Palestinian state.

There is no need to engage in one-sided analysis. The fault for the impasse in Israeli-Palestinian relations over the past seventy years lies with both sides and, at this late stage, the prospects for a two-state solution look gloomier than ever. But many diasporic Jews, myself included, are less than comfortable with an Israeli government that denies any legitimacy to Palestinian claims to a homeland of their own and refuses to enter into serious negotiations to resolve matters. Hence, a growing disenchantment among more liberal elements of world Jewry with a state whose behaviour is at odds with their own moral code.

Does it mean a withdrawal on their part of support for Israel's right to exist? Of course not. Nor does it entail dismissing the many obstacles to overcoming seventy years of hostility between two peoples — Ireland is there to remind us for just how long grievances can fester. But a shadow has been cast on the relations between mainstream Israel — the one represented by the religious parties and Likud — and significant parts of the diaspora, one that will not disappear tomorrow.

I have visited Israel on two occasions, one in the summer of 1966 when I spent a month in the company of European students from various countries working on a kibbutz in the Galilee, the other in the spring of 1995, when Yitzhak Rabin was prime minister and the peace process in full swing. I wish the hopefulness of that period could somehow return. Sadly, I won't hold my breath.

From my journal entries:

MAY 25, 1995, JERUSALEM: Sitting on the balcony of my hotel room in Jerusalem on my first night here. It is hot — a drier heat than Greece, if that is possible. The city has a beauty, especially the old city where I walked today, with its Jewish, Armenian, and Christian quarters and, high on the temple mount, the magnificent

Dome of the Rock. Religion is in the air, something unavoidable given the theological foundations of the three monotheistic faiths rooted in this city.

I am also conscious of the political realities of a country with roadblocks along the Tel Aviv-Jerusalem highway and line after line of Israeli settlements marking the boundaries of an enduring conflict.

MAY 26, 1995, JERUSALEM: The profound ambiguities that a stay in Jerusalem brings to the surface. A sense of the millennia of history as I made my way yesterday to the old city and the Wailing Wall. But a profound discomfort faced with the orthodox thrusting their phylacteries (Tefillin) at all and sundry, exploiting the religious potential of the site for all it is worth. Similarly, I can identify with the state of Israel and with the Jewish nature of West Jerusalem, yet feel profound discomfort with the large Israeli flag and menorah as one approaches the Via Dolorosa and the Damascus Gate or that adorn the Hyatt on the approach to Mount Scopus. The insensitivity of Israeli politicians to the Arab no less than Jewish nature of the city is all too palpable.

It is not that I expect Israelis to act angelically or to submerge their own quest for identity in recognition of that of the "other." But religious zeal of the type that underlies what I see in this city and nationalist zeal of the type that Likud and its supporters propagate betray the sort of values that Jews in the diaspora and even in the early days of the Zionist movement aspired to — justice, a measure of equality, solidarity towards one's own but also towards others.

What comes home on this trip is the degree to which Israel has become a Middle Eastern state, resonating to some of the same values one finds elsewhere in this region. There is undoubtedly religious fundamentalism, at one extreme, for example, in Mea She'arim and in many of the settlements. Nationalism *à l'outrance*, recalling the Greek position over Macedonia. The habits of hot climates — loud gestures, a greater informality in dress and appearance, a willingness to bend regulations and rules. But to these it brings a significant measure of Western values, not least a strong work ethic and a valorization of education, culture and research that catapults it into the ranks of the achievers in this world, along with Taiwan, South Korea, or Singapore. And there remains within Israeli political culture, on the left and in the universities, a tradition of secular humanism with which I can identify. All this to make me temper my judgements.

The reflections of two poets on Jerusalem, the first, Israeli, the second, Palestinian:

Yehuda Amichai: "Jerusalem, the only city in the world where the right to vote is granted even to the dead."

Tamim al-Barghouti: "In Jerusalem there's [everyone else] / Except for you / Let your eye not weep, young Arab / I see no one except for you."

JUNE 28, 2013, VANCOUVER: Margarethe von Trotta's *Hannah Arendt*. A bracing film that highlights the role of the critical intellectual. Should Eichmann have been on trial in Jerusalem in 1961 for crimes against the Jews or should he have been on trial as a horrendous example of crimes against humanity? What role does the philosopher have to play in interpreting events that beggar our imagination and weigh us down? Are the Eichmanns of this world monsters in and of themselves or banal examples of the imperative to follow orders within a scheme that has a closed logic of its own, the totalitarian one Arendt had so well described in her earlier book, *The Origins of Totalitarianism*?

·Can thinking save us from our worst excesses? Arendt sees this as a primary human function. At one level this is true, our ability to use reason and language as opposed to pure instinct or passion, unlike other living creatures. Yet she overdoes it. For even she is subject to her own passions — her love for Heidegger, her love for friends over people or nations.

In her reaction to the Eichmann trial, she is a cosmopolitan in the best sense of the word. Many of her closest friends will abandon her, following publication of *Eichmann in Jerusalem*, feeling that she has turned her back on her own people, that she lacks *ahavat Yisrael* (a love for her fellow Jews). But to dissent from the shibboleths of one's own community takes a kind of courage that only a tiny few can ever muster.

CHAPTER 2

The Springtime
of Peoples

I CAME OF AGE at the same time as Quebec. With Maurice
Duplessis' death in September 1959, a new era began. Films which
had been banned, for example Ingmar Bergman's *The Seventh Seal*,
could suddenly be screened. Universities which had not been able
to touch funds for higher education allocated by the federal government would now be able to do so under a new agreement. There
was a whiff of springtime in the air, much like the thaw which had
followed Stalin's death in the USSR.

Things began to speed up dramatically with the victory of the
Quebec Liberal Party under Jean Lesage in the 1960 provincial
election. Quebec, which had been very much the laggard where
social spending was concerned, was now in a catch-up mode. The
Church, which had dominated the education of French Canadians
ever since Confederation, was about to lose its stranglehold. And

following the 1962 election, the Quebec government would proceed to nationalize the Anglo-controlled private electricity companies, so that Quebecers could become "masters in their own home."

These changes bespoke a new nationalism, which would see
Quebec governments increasingly at odds with the federal one. For
not only would the newly empowered provincial government be
fighting Ottawa for access to tax revenue to finance its programs,
but there was an undercurrent in Quebec society, influenced by the
wave of decolonization from abroad. After all, if Cuba could defy
the American giant in the aftermath of its revolution, and the
Algerians the French in achieving their independence, why should
Quebec trail behind?

Such was the spirit which led French Canadian university students to march in their thousands in 1962 to demand the resigna-
tion of Donald Gordon, president of the publicly-owned Canadian
National Railway, who had claimed there were no French Canadians
with the competence to serve on its board of directors. Or newly
established separatist parties like the Rassemblement pour l'in-
dépendance nationale to instigate a riot during the visit of Queen
Elizabeth II to Quebec City in 1964. Or more ominously yet, the
Front de libération du Québec to begin a series of mailbox explo-
sions and attacks on federal armouries culminating in the kidnap-
ping of James Cross, the British trade commissioner in Montreal,
and of Pierre Laporte, a leading provincial cabinet minister (subsequently murdered) in the so-called October Crisis of 1970.

It was hard to ignore the signals. As an undergraduate student
at McGill in the early 1960s, I found myself groping for an understanding of the new Quebec. The very first political commentary I
ever penned was a one-page leaflet for McGill's New Democratic
Party Club entitled "An Austro-Hungarian Solution for Canada."
If my memory serves me right, in my naïveté I saw in the confed-

eral arrangement that had characterized the relations between Austria and Hungary after 1867, coupled with a fair degree of cultural autonomy to the other nationalities of the Austro-Hungarian empire, a possible future model for Canada. (We had no Franz Joseph, mind you, to try to keep the unwieldy structure together!)

This turned out to be the beginning of a life-long interest in the fate not only of Quebec, but of minority-type nations like Quebec and of the larger multinational states of which they were a part. On graduating from McGill in 1965, I was awarded a two-year fellowship allowing me to spend the first year at the Institut d'études politiques (Sciences Po) in Paris, with the second in the MA program back at McGill. Among other things, the year in Paris allowed me to achieve a level of proficiency in French significantly above the standard for anglophone Montrealers of the day and to cultivate the friendship of a number of French Canadians for the first time.

Strange to say, but Paris constituted a sort of neutral ground between the two Canadian solitudes. For, as French Canadians who had come to France with the expectation of being welcomed with open arms were to discover, their French counterparts often treated them with their odd diction (so unlike Parisian French!) with considerable disdain. Suddenly, Anglos from back home, especially if they were able to communicate in French, were potential friends.

I was to experience a second full year in Paris in 1969–70, by which time I was in the PhD program at the University of Toronto. This was in the immediate aftermath of the May 1968 events and the atmosphere was still highly charged. Needless to say, most of my friends were on the student left and this included no small number of Québécois, as French Canadians had by now come to be called.

My return to Toronto in the fall of 1970 coincided with the October Crisis. Along with some fellow students at U of T and with the assistance of allies on the student newspaper, *The Varsity*, we proceeded to print a large broadside with the title "Quebec Occupied," following the invocation of the War Measures Act by the Trudeau government. Since no Toronto printer would touch this in the crisis atmosphere then prevailing, we had it printed in Buffalo and proceeded to plaster it on bank facades and other structures in a midnight pasting foray. We also organized a teach-in on Quebec in a downtown church some weeks later, inviting radical Québécois figures of the day like Jean-Marc Piotte.

The point of the above is not to underline our romantic heroism, or, critics would say, folly. Rather, it suggested that some in English Canada were not prepared to buy into the hysteria being promoted by both the federal government and the media, showing instead considerable sympathy for the current of progressive nationalism emerging in Quebec at that time, though not for the terrorist tactics of the FLQ.

In my case, the sympathy would carry over into the first term of the Lévesque government, following the Parti Québécois' surprising electoral victory in 1976. By then I was a young faculty member in the Political Science department at the University of British Columbia, teaching among other things a course on Quebec politics. Bill 101, the so-called Charter of the French Language, entrenched the position of French as the dominant language in Quebec, and began the process of channelling the children of new immigrants to Quebec into French-language rather than English-language schools — *les enfants de la loi 101*, as they came to be known subsequently. The PQ government also passed the most stringent legislation to control contributions to political parties of any jurisdiction in North America and very tough anti-scab legislation, where labour disputes were concerned. In short, it was a progressive government in a number of respects and René Lévesque an appealing figure.

The referendum of 1980 on sovereignty-association brought the question of Quebec's relationship to the rest of Canada to a head. Had the referendum passed, Quebec would have become a sovereign state, albeit with some ongoing association with the rest of Canada, if English Canada had been prepared to go along. (By no means a sure bet!) Canada, in turn, would have found itself with its Atlantic provinces physically separated from the rest of the country — a kind of East Pakistan with a sovereign Quebec as its immediate neighbour. Not an impossible arrangement, assuming amicable relations between a sovereign Quebec and Canada, but hardly the stuff of dreams for a country whose underlying mythos spoke of a single political nationality from sea to sea.

In the event, the Sovereignty-Association referendum in Quebec failed by a margin of 3–2, roughly 40 percent voting in its favour and 60 percent against. The forceful intervention of Pierre Trudeau in opposition to the proposal played a seminal role in countering the appeal of Lévesque and others to Quebec nationalism. At the time, had I been living in Quebec, I would have been voting on the Yes side. By the time of the second referendum in 1995 on Sovereignty-Partnership, I would have been on the side of the No.

Why might this be so? I need to go back to my graduate student years in Toronto for an explanation. The late 1960s was a heady time, not only in Quebec, but in English-speaking Canada as well. A new nationalism was in the air, channelled by groups like the Committee for an Independent Canada and the Waffle within the NDP. There was concern about excessive foreign (read American) ownership of the Canadian economy — the Watkins report of 1968 comes to mind. The same was true regarding Canadian unions, often branch plants of American ones. And there was significant alarm about the degree to which Canadian media and culture at large had come to be dominated by the United States.

The Vietnam War had turned significant sections of Canadian public opinion against the prevailing pro-American stance in our foreign policy implanted during the Cold War. The flood of draft dodgers fleeing to Canada also played a role. So that Canadian nationalism, as its proponents saw it, bespoke a greater degree of independence vis-à-vis the United States and the American empire at large.

That was certainly the gist of my own academic writing in those years, both my MA thesis for McGill on Canadian Defence Policy and the American Empire and my eventual PhD thesis at U of T entitled "The Land of Cain: Class and Nationalism in English Canada 1945–1975." While I was without a doubt supportive of a progressive Quebec nationalism, I was no less supportive of a progressive English-Canadian one.

Would these two eventually prove incompatible? It was not obvious to me at the time, but then English Canada was experiencing its own version of a springtime of the people, so why emphasize potential conflicts between the two? But slowly, as the 1980s unfolded, I would become more conscious of the limitations of Quebec nationalism and of the complexities that the Canada-Quebec relationship entailed.

The second term of the PQ, following on the loss of the 1980 referendum, turned out to be a lot less progressive than the first, with major conflicts with Quebec's trade unions dominating the agenda. And with the return to power of the Quebec Liberals under Robert Bourassa, the new refrain would be one of Quebec Inc., favouring the emergence of a stronger Quebec-based capitalism rather than any alternative model.

At the federal level, the Canadian nationalism of the late 1960s and early 1970s was giving way to a quite different turn by the 1980s, in the direction of free trade with the United States. Canadian big business, not least its powerful banks, was far more interested in the potential of the larger American market than in promoting Canadian ownership at home. And the government of Brian Mulroney would do everything in its power to achieve this, culminating in the Canada-US Free Trade Agreement of 1988.

Like many on the liberal-left, I saw in these developments a serious undermining of Canadian sovereignty and a move towards a much more market-dominated vision of society. At the same time, the Mulroney government was pursuing a more decentralizing version of federalism through the so-called Meech Lake Accord. Its main purpose was to get Quebec to assent to the patriation of the Canadian constitution that had been engineered by Pierre Trudeau in 1982 over the opposition of the Lévesque government. The problem from my perspective was that the Meech Lake Accord weakened the federal government by giving more power to the provinces, something which ran against my own commitment to a reasonably strong central government and a robust form of Canadian identity that was more than the sum of ten provincial ones.

A key factor in the re-election of the Mulroney government in November 1988 and the ratification of the Free Trade Agreement was the support the Conservatives garnered in Quebec, not only from Robert Bourassa but from the PQ as well. For all their reputed nationalism, Québécois were more prepared to play the American card than were their English Canadian counterparts.

I wrote a book-length essay, *Letters to a Québécois Friend*, shortly after the election. In it I vented my indignation at the turn of events, castigating Québécois nationalists for their short-sightedness where the American colossus was concerned and expressing my resentment of the Bourassa government's attempts *à la* Meech Lake to weaken the federal government. I was beginning to learn firsthand just how fraught the relations between majority and minority nationalities in a multinational state could be.

My essay was published with a retort from Daniel Latouche and became part of the ensuing fracas surrounding the collapse of the Meech Lake Accord in June 1990. I had had my baptism by fire and would consecrate a fair amount of my time and energy in the immediate years that followed to the evolving Canada-Quebec debate.

In 1991 I published another book-length essay, *Toward a Canada-Quebec Union*, looking toward a possible confederal arrangement between English Canada and Quebec with a good deal of autonomy to each component, should the Canadian federation fail. In 1994 came one more book-length essay, *Thinking English Canada*, seeking to map the components of English Canadian identity, in contradistinction from Quebec's. These included a political mixture of conservatism, liberalism and socialism, a strong sense of regionalism, and acknowledgment of both the aboriginal and multicultural components in the equation.

The most difficult task I discovered, in media interventions following publication of the book, was winning acceptance for the term English Canada. Not only was there controversy about the exact meaning of the term English — this in an increasingly multicultural society — but an overwhelming majority of those living outside Quebec thought of themselves as Canadian by nationality, rather than English Canadian. There really was no English Canadian nationality, even in the sociological sense that I had intended, in the way there clearly was a Québécois one.

The politics of constitutional reform continued thick and fast through to 1992, the time of the Charlottetown Accord. Although endorsed by the federal government, all ten premiers, and the three major federal political parties of the day, this mega-constitutional package with multiple components fell afoul of majority opinion across the country. If Quebec sovereigntists and soft nationalists voted against it because it didn't go far enough, its opponents in English-speaking Canada, especially in the West, opposed what they saw as excessive concessions to Quebec, in particular the guarantee of a permanent 25 percent of House of Commons seats for a province with a diminishing share of the overall population. (This was meant to be balanced out by Quebec's acceptance of a Senate with equal representation from all ten provinces, unlike the existing Upper Chamber.) With 55 percent of the electorate voting against Charlottetown in the October 1992 referendum, constitutional reform or the tarnished "C" word vanished from the political agenda overnight.

That was not quite the end of the Canada-Quebec *danse-à-deux*. The federal election of 1993 saw the hollowing out of both the Conservatives and the NDP, with the emergence of two new parties, Reform in Western Canada and the Bloc Québécois in Quebec, with mutually exclusive agendas. The next year saw the return of the PQ to power in 1994, followed by a second referendum on Quebec sovereignty. This came in the fall of 1995, with Lucien Bouchard, leader of the Bloc Québécois, providing much of the dynamism on the pro-sovereignty side, against a weaker array of pro-federalist Quebec politicians. In the event, the No side scraped by with a bare 50.6 percent of the vote against 49.4 percent for the Yes.

What would have happened had the Yes side actually won? It seems as though Jacques Parizeau, the PQ premier of Quebec, would have declared sovereignty immediately. He might also have found a willing ally in Jacques Chirac, the president of France. But the upshot would have been one big mess. The Cree in northern Quebec would have declared their intention to remain part of Canada. The nine other Canadian provinces and the ensuing federal government (presumably with a prime minister other than Jean Chrétien) would have played very tough regarding negotiations with Quebec on any future partnership. The Canadian dollar would have been devalued and the flight of capital from Quebec impossible to contain.

Like many other Canadians, I was a keen observer of all this. I even had a privileged position of sorts as a weekly columnist for the Montreal newspaper *Le Devoir* during the 1995 referendum year. While I was carefully nuanced in my interventions on the referendum, I had by now become less enamoured of the sovereignty cause than back in 1980. I found there was a fair amount of demagoguery to Bouchard's appeal, while Parizeau was haughty and imperious when compared to a much more affable René Lévesque. More to the point, there was nothing very romantic about Quebec nationalism by 1995 and lots of reasons following the breakup of the USSR, Czechoslovakia, and especially Yugoslavia to fear the potential for disruption and even violence were Canada to follow suit.

Subsequently, the Supreme Court of Canada, following a referral from the federal government, was to lay down a series of guidelines to regulate any future referenda on sovereignty. These became the basis for the Clarity Act of 2000, limiting the ability of any future Quebec government to set the terms for any such referendum on its own. And in 2006, in a surprise move, the Harper government introduced a motion in the House of Commons recognizing the Québécois as constituting a nation within a united Canada, symbolic recognition of a sort for Quebec's distinctive national character. That is where matters stand at the moment, with the sovereignty question very much on the back burner in Quebec.

There was clearly a generational element to the sovereignty movement. And it is also the case that one cannot hold referenda on something as polarizing as sovereignty on a recurring basis. It is to the credit of both Canada and Quebec that the issue was put to referendum on two occasions and that all sides were prepared to see the process as legitimate, something most other countries with minority nationalities would not be willing to do. That is one lesson I would draw from our experience.

My interest in the Canada-Quebec relationship would lead me to seek comparisons elsewhere. The most obvious ones were a number of West European countries with similar majority-minority nationality differences. The ones I came to focus on were Spain, Belgium, and the United Kingdom. And I would have occasion to spend some time in each.

In the Spanish case, Catalonia bore the most direct parallel with Quebec; for example, there had been contact between Catalonia and Quebec's Office de la langue française regarding guidelines for the enhanced use of Catalan as opposed to Spanish in that region. The Basque Country was another possible comparison point, though the violence perpetrated by the Euskadi Ta Askatasuna (ETA) in the aftermath of Spain's transition to democracy far exceeded what the FLQ was ever able to carry out. (It was only in 2018 that ETA's leadership, often sequestered in France, announced its official dissolution.)

Spain had established a Statute of Autonomy for its seventeen regions in the post-Franco period and had recognized the linguistic specificity of Catalonia, the Basque Country, and Galicia in the process. For about twenty-five years, the new arrangement worked reasonably well. But by 2004, the Catalans whose share of the contribution to the central government's overall revenue they considered excessive were chafing at the bit, demanding a greater degree of autonomy. A new arrangement was worked out with the then Socialist government of Spain, including several references to Catalonia's national character. This was too much for Spain's Constitutional court, whose conservative majority threw out offending portions of the revised Statute in 2010.

This decision was like waving a red cloth in front of a bull, provoking a wave of Catalan nationalism that would eventually lead to a loose alliance of Catalan parties seeking an independence referendum from Spain. The Spanish constitution, while recognizing minority nationalities, speaks of Spain's indissoluble unity and leaves recourse to any binding referenda in the hands of the central government. This was something Spain's conservative government was unwilling to undertake, and a game of cat and mouse began between Madrid and would-be secessionist governments in Catalonia, culminating in the proclamation of Article 155, central government rule over Catalonia, from October 2017 to June 2018. Where things will go in the future remains to be seen, with public opinion in Catalonia sharply divided between those favouring independence and those opposed.

In the case of Belgium, referenda are off the table. But the divisions between the majority Flemish-speaking region and the minority French-speaking Walloon region are palpable, with largely French-speaking Brussels (coincidentally the headquarters of the European Union and the European Commission) a major bone of contention between the two. It is the Flemish, historically dominated by their French-speaking counterparts, who have pushed the case for ever greater decentralization of the country, all the more since they have been the more prosperous region in the post-World War II period. There have been successive separatist parties in Flanders, and while Belgium hangs together, it is a weak conglomeration of three regions, Flanders, Wallonia, and Brussels, with a hollowed-out central government.

In the case of the United Kingdom, both Scotland and Wales achieved devolution from Westminster following referenda in 1997, with the Scottish Assembly acquiring greater powers than the Welsh one. The Scottish National Party (analogous to the PQ) became the governing party of Scotland in 2007. Once it had acquired a legislative majority in 2011, it pressed for a referendum on independence. This was eventually agreed to by the U.K. government, but with a much clearer question on the ballot than Quebec's fudging of sovereignty with association or partnership in its two referenda. A referendum was held in October 2014 on the question, "Should Scotland be an Independent Country?" with 45 percent voting in favour and 55 percent against.

So, much like in Quebec, the question of Scottish independence seemed relegated to the back burner. But Brexit has revived deep divisions, with Scotland voting strongly to remain in the European Union in 2016, and England and Wales voting to leave. If nothing else, this ensures that the question of Scottish nationalism will not simply vanish into the mist.

In all these cases we are dealing with the attempted break-up of long-established states. Many within the minority nationalities (or in the case of Belgium, within the majority Flemish nationality with some of the reflexes of a former minority) see themselves as constituting an "almost country" of their own. Historical, linguistic, economic, and institutional characteristics help shape this sentiment, with political parties and leaders seeking to channel it. How the majority nationality and/or the central government react to such demands over time often determines the ultimate outcome.

Over the years, I have written a fair amount on the dialectic at play between majority and minority nationalities within multinational states. I have tried to highlight a number of tendencies. The first is the tension between the desire for recognition by minority nationalities and the *ressentiment* these claims can provoke from majority nationalities when they see these as excessive. The second would be a desire for a looser more confederal type arrangement by minority nationalities and for a more centralized or classically federal one on the part of majority ones. The third is the hubris which has often characterized the attitude of majority nationalities through history, particularly when they commanded overseas empires (think of the Castilians or the English). The fourth is a corresponding melancholy in the outlook of minority nationalities (think of the Scots, the Catalans, or the Québécois who recall defeats more easily than victories). And finally, there are conflicting views of what constitutes the national history of one's country and of key moments in its development.

In the process of studying them, I have become more aware of the potential fragility of multinational federations and more convinced of the importance of preserving them. To the degree that they recognize legitimate claims to political autonomy and linguistic security for their minority nationalities, they meet key democratic criteria. To the degree that they may even permit the occasional referendum on sovereignty, even more so. One of the great strengths of multinational federations is that while acknowledging national differences within their borders, they put constraints on just how far that nationalism will go, both for the majority and the minority. No small matter in a world where nationalism, even in the twenty-first century, has too often turned out to be a baleful force. With the ripeness of years I am much more conscious of the Janus-like character of nationalism, one face affirming the positive characteristics of a particular nationality or group, the other hostile and intolerant towards anything which might restrict it. It is the first face, not the second, which we need to preserve.

Some journal entries:

DEC. 17, 1988, VANCOUVER: I have begun writing an essay tentatively entitled *Letters to a Québécois Friend*. An attempt to work out my reaction to the Nov. 21st election that will bring us free trade with the United States, and in the process complicate the relations between our two Canadian solitudes. I am aggrieved by the way Quebec has voted, by its embrace of North American continentalism and an unbridled capitalist ethos. And I am terribly uncertain as to what will happen to Canada as a whole in the aftermath.

OCT. 10, 1993, QUEBEC CITY: A colloquium at Laval University on *Identité et Modernité*. A model of pluralism and openness that would have done any English Canadian university proud. Quebec nationalism is beginning to lose its intolerant edge, certainly in the academic world, and probably beyond. There is growing recognition of international connections at all levels and that closed-mindedness goes poorly with open borders. A *Québec des citoyens* is a very different proposition from the *Québec pure laine* of yesteryear. And I detect a greater openness to bridges to English Canada than before.

FEB., 2000, BRUSSELS: My little studio apartment for a month. I am not unhappy here, despite the rains that come in the afternoon and the overcast sky that sings of Jacques Brel.

Is there a single Belgian history? Is there a single Canadian one? Spanish? British? What does it mean to re-think history along multinational lines? What does it leave by way of shared history, what does it sweep away?

Serge Jaumain, a colleague who did his graduate work in Canada, told me the other day how much more together Canada seems to him as a country as compared to Belgium, how deeply self-doubting Belgians tend to be. And I had felt that Canadians were a self-doubting bunch, particularly face to face with the United States.

A long chat with a law professor, Hugues Dumont, yesterday. He likes my *ressentiment* theme, gives me examples of this even in the internal relations between Walloons and French-speaking Brussels. He insists that there is only a truce where Flemish-French relations are concerned, that a number of issues from the Statute of Brussels to social security are ticking bombs. Belgium may be able to pull through in the future, but there is the danger of *la coquille vide*, an empty shell where the powers of the central government are concerned, if the logic of confederalism wins out.

In this regard, the political philosopher, Philippe Van Parijs's manuscript, *La Grande et Ultime Tâche de la Belgique*, which he lets me read, is also highly revealing. The logic is confederal through and through, with Flanders and Wallonia going their largely separate ways. Is there still a common will left over to be Belgian? Van Parijs seems to think not, though he may be misreading popular sentiment on the Flemish side, as the survey data I have seen would suggest. But the substance of Flemish nationalism presses towards confederal-type arrangements, as one of the leading Flemish parties, the Volksunie, openly proposes, and Luc van den Brande, a former minister-president of the Flemish government, seeks.

Melancholy as a prevailing theme in minority nationalities: I first encounter this in reading about the Basque case. But one finds it in Scotland, in Quebec — *être né pour un petit pain* — and plentifully in Wallonia. And not only among minority nationalities. George Grant articulated it for English Canada with his *Lament for a Nation*, much as did some of our writers, e.g. Margaret Atwood in *Survival* and Leonard Cohen in *Beautiful Losers*.

The long and short is that I leave Brussels for home much the richer for my visit, confident that I am on to something in trying to map the competing nationalisms one finds in multinational states.

CHAPTER 3

The Many Guises
of the Left

STARTING WITH MY adolescent years, I found myself attracted to the left. I am not quite sure how this originated. My parents, like many immigrants of their generation, voted Liberal, nor were there any notable left-wingers in my immediate milieu. But as I became politically conscious, I gravitated leftwards. Not to the hard left associated with the Communist Party, which had its adepts in Canada, albeit few in numbers. But to the social democratic left associated with the Labour Party in the U.K., its Socialist counterparts on the continent and elsewhere, and here at home with the newly formed New Democratic Party whose student club I joined upon entering McGill.

The 1960s turned out to be an ideal time to be on the left. In Canada, reform was in the air, not only in Quebec with the Quiet Revolution underway, but in Saskatchewan whose CCF/NDP government pioneered Medicare, and at the federal level where the Canada Pension Plan and a Canada-wide Medicare program were major achievements of the Pearson government. As a McGill student, I had been one of many canvassers for Charles Taylor, my popular political theory professor who would go on to become a leading communitarian-inclined philosopher of our day, when he ran unsuccessfully for the NDP in the federal riding of Mount Royal. And as echoes of student protests from faraway Berkeley reached our ears, student politics would become more passionate in Canada as well.

Going off to Paris in 1965–66, I found myself immersed in an intellectual milieu quite unlike Canada's. Sartre was still alive, and though existentialism had lost its cutting edge, his public stances on issues of the day mattered. Structuralism was the new flavour of the era in the social sciences, and there was a strongly Marxist undercurrent to intellectual and political debates and to French academic life. I found myself gravitating towards a disciple of Georg Lukács, Lucien Goldmann, a sociologist of literature, whose key book, *The Hidden God*, had been a class analysis of the writings of such eminent French authors of *le grand siècle* as Pascal and Racine. But the humanist Marxism that Goldmann advocated, with its emphasis on the works of the young Marx and their evocation of alienation, was a far cry from the so-called scientific Marxism of Louis Althusser, the guru of the École normale supérieure, with his emphasis on Marx's post-1848 writings, especially on his *Capital*. Heady stuff for a twenty-one year-old trying to navigate unfamiliar waters.

By the time of my return to Canada, I had become part and parcel of an emerging new left. It was in Toronto, where I moved in the Expo year of 1967, that I would eventually become a student activist. Not before a one-year stint as a researcher on a CBC TV public affairs program, *The Way It Is*, where careers were on the make and the office politics feral. If nothing else, my year at the CBC taught me to be comfortable with the media, a skill that would prove helpful on a number of future occasions.

I entered the PhD program at U of T in 1968 and helped organize an activist group known as the Toronto Student Movement. Its focus was on enhancing student power within the university, seeking links with unions and workers outside, and aiming at wholesale change in Canadian society at large. The Vietnam War and Canada's ongoing links with the American military establishment were a major target.

Two particular events during that period stick in my mind. One was the decision to join striking journalists on the picket lines at the Peterborough newspaper, an action resulting in the arrest of a number of the students. And the other, which received a good deal of media attention, was the decision to disrupt a speech by Clark Kerr, former president of the University of California, in the Auditorium of the Royal Ontario Museum in the presence of Claude Bissell, president of U of T, and other university bigwigs. Kerr was associated with the concept of the multiversity and in our eyes this represented the move towards a more corporate-oriented university, rather than the critical university we advocated.

Halfway through his speech a few of us mounted the stage and engaged in a form of guerrilla theatre. If my memory serves me right, we then let him finish his speech — it had never been our intention to prevent him from speaking in the first place — but our point had been made. And we celebrated afterwards in '60s style, "Sympathy for the Devil," "Come on Baby, Light my Fire," and marijuana wafting through an apartment in nearby Rochdale College. This was a co-op residence whose name had been borrowed from the first co-operative movement established in mid-nineteenth century Rochdale, England, and which, in its Bloor Street incarnation, had become a haven for the counterculture.

Where might all this lead? The previous year had seen momentous events in France when the May 1968 events had almost brought down the regime of Charles de Gaulle. In West Germany, the extra-parliamentary opposition was taking aim at the complicity of an older generation with Nazism and at the presence of American bases in the country, even as napalm bombs were being dropped on innocent civilians in Vietnam. In the United States four students were to lose their lives at Kent State in 1970 during anti-war protests. "The natives are restless," one slogan put it. "Don't trust anyone over 30," was another. And perhaps the most famous of the period, emanating from Paris, "It is forbidden to forbid."

The student activism of the 1960s would prove a passing phase. True, Lyndon Johnson was unable to seek a second term as president and eventually the Americans were forced to retreat from Vietnam in their first-ever military defeat. The Gaullist regime was shaken, but came back to carry the day. Extra-parliamentary opposition could rally supporters in the initial stages of a popular movement, but in the long run institutional structures, including familiar parliamentary and electoral ones, would triumph.

Yet not all was in vain. Universities throughout the Western world, including Canadian ones, opened their doors to greater student participation at all levels of decision-making. Movements for women's liberation, for gay liberation, for the rights of Indigenous peoples had their roots in the activism of the 1960s. And there would be protest movements again, for example against the arms race in the 1980s or the pending Iraq war in 2003, that would bring millions into the streets of Western cities.

By the 1970s, however, the mood had shifted drastically and

with it the high hopes for change that many in the '60s had entertained. *Les Trente Glorieuses* as they came to be known in French, the long post-war boom which had brought rising salaries and a capacious welfare state to most Western countries, were at an end. Keynesianism, of which Canada had been one of the very first champions as far back as 1945, was about to be displaced by monetarism, and the turn to neo-liberal economic policies. Privatization of state-owned enterprises, attacks on trade unions, cutbacks in welfare spending were now the norm, associated with names like Margaret Thatcher and Ronald Reagan and with well-funded research institutes (Institute for Economic Affairs, Cato, Fraser) pushing for ever-greater market freedom. All this would be amplified through bodies like the G7, GATT, or the OECD, preaching the new gospel to countries of the South.

More momentous changes yet were in the wings. The coming to power in the Soviet Union of Mikhail Gorbachev in 1985 was to totally transform the international order. What began as long overdue attempts to reform a moribund system, cemented by forty years of Cold War, would lead from *glasnost* and *perestroika* to the break-up of the Soviet Union itself and the freeing of the countries of Eastern Europe from Soviet control. The symbolic highpoint for this was the tearing down of the Berlin Wall in November 1989, and the reunification of Germany. Ideologically what this spelled was the collapse of Soviet-style communism as the major rival to Western capitalism.

I had never been an adherent of the Soviet system. I had studied it in university, had read a good deal by way of Russian and Soviet history, and had had occasion to visit the country briefly, first as a student in 1965 and then as a delegate to an international political science congress in 1979. Quite aside from its bureaucratic heaviness and economic inefficiency, the absence of political freedom was its most glaring defect. The Stalin years had been particularly horrendous as the dissident literature that came flooding into the west — Aleksandr Solzhenitsyn, Vasily Grossman — was to show. But long before that Arthur Koestler had exposed the mechanism of the 1930s purge trials in *Darkness at Noon* and George Orwell the perverse nature of the regime both in *Animal Farm* and *1984*.

While I saw myself as a socialist, it was in the Western mould, with due respect for democratic practices and individual rights. The Leninist practice of substituting the will of a vanguard party for that of the people offended me to the quick, much as it had offended my great heroine, Rosa Luxemburg, back in 1918. And what was true for the Soviet Union was no less true for China, where Mao had sacrificed tens of millions in the follies, which were the Great Leap Forward and the Cultural Revolution.

So what would become of the left in the aftermath of the Soviet meltdown? And what sort of future did I see for socialism in the era of global capitalism?

In the short-run, social democratic parties were not too badly affected by the events of 1989. It was communist parties in the west which went into free fall and never recovered. But the removal of the communist bogey, so to speak, had the perverse effect of reinforcing the claims of the most hardened supporters of capitalism to be the only viable game in town and to press even harder for tax cuts to benefit corporations and the wealthy at the expense of the bottom 80 percent of society. It is not by chance, as Thomas Piketty among others was to show, that salaries began to stagnate in this period as trade unions lost membership, even as the beneficiaries of high finance and stock offerings prospered. With global capitalism the new flavour of the era, social democratic parties would either have to play the game like their political rivals to the right or begin to haemorrhage support.

In the event, parties like Labour in Britain under Tony Blair or the SPD in Germany under Gerhard Schröder shifted to the right, becoming pale images of the parties which had once represented working class interests. Blair was on intimate terms with the ruthlessly right-wing media baron, Rupert Murdoch, and far more interested in turning London into a flagship of global capitalism than in addressing the inequalities in British society. Schröder, for his part, forced major wage concessions onto German trade unions for apprentices and young workers in the name of enhanced economic competitiveness. The era of short-term contracts, low wages, and minimal job security — the precariat as sociologists have come to call such employees — was on its way.

A major factor in this realignment of values was the emergence of new poles of global capitalism, especially in East Asia. While the take-off of post-war Japan and eventually Taiwan, South Korea, and Singapore was by now old hat, the transformation of China from a Marxist-Leninist to a market-Leninist society following the ascension of Deng Xiaoping was dramatic. Within four decades, China would become the manufacturing centre of the global economy and a major contender for global hegemony with the United States. In the process, industrial jobs in the Western world were to take a nose-dive.

Social democratic parties found themselves playing rearguard defence in what was a tilted playing field. There was not much they could do, even in office, to prevent the transfer of jobs overseas, or the replacement of relatively secure high-paying jobs by low-paying insecure ones. Nor could they resort to significantly higher taxation on the wealthy and corporations, for fear of losing their country's all-important credit rating with international agencies, thus inducing a possible flight of capital. Their electoral support began to wither on the vine.

My thesis advisor at U of T had been C.B. Macpherson, a political theorist best known for his book *The Political Theory of Possessive Individualism: Hobbes to Locke*. While Macpherson had tried to trace the emergence of the key attributes of a market society with the attendant values of unlimited accumulation as far back as seventeenth-century England, in some ways he was the prophet of the new era we had now entered. In global capitalism unlimited accumulation was the norm. As one adage put it, "Eat lunch or be lunch." And those values in turn, through the enormous powers of advertising, emulation, and political indoctrination — "there is no alternative" — became the prevailing norms of societies around the world.

In the aftermath of communism's collapse, socialism appeared to its critics to be the graveyard of misplaced hopes. But capitalism, in turn, was to prove the harbinger of globalized excess, subject to periodic financial crises, as in 2008, and opening the door to long-term ecological catastrophes. Moreover, the Social Darwinism, which its more extreme supporters promoted, a dog-eat-dog mentality, could only undercut the fabric of societies around the world. But then Margaret Thatcher had once famously proclaimed, "There is no such thing as society," so neo-liberals with their possessive individualist ethos had no reason to lament its weakening.

Let me return to Marx for a moment, not the Marx who had been turned into an icon in the Marxist-Leninist regimes of the twentieth century, but the critic of capitalism back in the nineteenth. What Marx did see clearly was both the creative and innovative character of capitalism and its tendency to breed exploitation and inequality in the process. And though his blueprint for a communist society to replace it was half-baked (to be charitable), his analysis of capitalism's defects remains extremely pertinent. Hence the continued interest in his work, a good two centuries after his birth.

This brings me to the question of the fate of socialism in the twenty-first century. There will be no quick-and-easy passageway from capitalism to socialism, as Marx and his twentieth- and twenty-first-century disciples might have hoped. In fact, capitalism in its globalizing form still has a long run ahead of it — though global warming may prove a greater threat to its long-term survival than a militant working class. Still, all is not well in the world of unlimited capitalist accumulation, and the inequality which capitalism engenders as a matter of course will provoke pushback.

There will be calls for regulation of technologies out of control and for greater redistribution from the beneficiaries of the brave new world of algorithm-trading capitalism and artificial intelligence to the many losers who fall by the wayside. Once again the state, so maligned by the right in recent decades, will be invoked to step into the breach. And a socialist or social democratic left will have an important contribution to make to this debate.

But for the left to be contemporary in its appeal it will also have to look in its own mirror. Even as the right was calling the shots economically and politically over the past three decades, the left slipped into its favourite fault-line position — internal divisions. Not the old ones between communists and socialists, Trotskyists or anarchists — the list could go on and on — but ones associated with identity politics.

It is one thing for various movements to advocate for their particular causes or constituencies. But when these constituencies talk past each other rather than to each other, when they see little in common with others who may also have to face the consequences of society's shortcomings and failures, the possibilities for collective action are much reduced. If all that matters is one's identity defined by gender, race, ethnicity, sexual orientation, or what have you, to the exclusion of anything else then the big-tent politics that socialism has historically stood for becomes impossible. That is one of the great challenges socialist parties in the Western world face at the moment.

Another one stems from the evolution of global capitalism and the crisis of immigration, especially into Europe, from countries of the South. Historically, socialism was internationalist in character and believed in solidarity across national lines, not only between workers but between nations. That spirit is significantly weakened at the moment as a result of the wholesale movement of would-be migrants from the South and the simultaneous disappearance of well-paying jobs in the North. The backlash against migration has seen the emergence of populist movements on the right in various European countries, support for Brexit in many traditionally Labour-leaning constituencies in England's former industrial heartland and in an analogous way, significant support for Trump in the American rust-belt states.

The challenge the left needs to face is the fact that solidarity is much stronger at the nation-state level than internationally, and is sometimes stronger at the regional level than within nation-states, and sometimes stronger at the local or municipal level. This means that there are finite limits to how far states can go in accepting wholesale migration from abroad, limits which even countries like Canada with a long history of immigration have had to recognize. At best, international solidarity is incremental in character, something that can be built onto the prevailing structure of national and sub-national solidarity, but without displacing it. The European Union, for all the best intentions of its founding fathers, is now struggling with this very dilemma, faced with would-be migrants in the millions from countries of the global South and with internal cleavages between its founding members and some of its more recent East European ones.

Let me add one parting thought to this discussion of challenges facing the twenty-first-century left, a slightly more positive one. Historically the left has had a utopian dimension to it, a faith that the world could be remade in a more egalitarian way and that shared interests could win out over purely individualistic ones. This remains a noble ideal and it would be one that the left would be foolish to discard.

In the spring of 2012, a wave of student protests swept Quebec, the so-called *printemps érable*. The main focus of concern was a threatened increase by the Quebec government to tuition fees, a familiar enough issue, although in Quebec university fees, as it turns out, were significantly lower than those elsewhere in Canada. But what caught my eye, observing the phenomenon from afar, was one of the slogans the students chanted as they marched through residential streets in Montreal one evening, banging pots and pans: "If you won't let us dream, we won't let you sleep."

That reminded me of the heady days of the student left back in the 1960s, of the romantic spirit that gripped many in my generation at the time. But the author of this memoir is no longer the young man he once was, and he is — perhaps sadly, perhaps wisely — conscious of the fact that, in the end, utopian ideals have to be feasible. This is even more true when one envisages the politics socialist parties can undertake when they actually achieve power. We need to think in terms of a feasible socialism in the real world of the twenty-first century with all the contradictions and challenges policy-making implies, rather than in terms of some ideal socialism that will never see the light of day. At the minimum, this entails accepting the reality of a mixed economy in which the market sector plays the leading economic role but state intervention and regulation coupled with a moderately redistributive tax system play an equally important balancing role — and one in which environmental concerns loom much larger than before.

CHAPTER 4

European
Reveries

IN MY CHILDHOOD imagination, Europe was a mysterious and far-off place: the scene of stories my mother would tell me, the setting for the fairy tales and novels that I came to read. Some day, perhaps, I would go there too. For the moment, while growing up in Montreal, there was only the St. Lawrence River, with its harbour and its ships, broadening as it flowed downstream into the Atlantic, pointing towards Europe's distant shores.

I would set foot in the Old World at the end of my second year at McGill, when I found myself on a chartered student flight heading to Europe for the summer. After a few days in London and a few more in Paris, I set off by train for my ultimate destination, Barcelona. As a student in political science and economics, I had joined an organization called AIESEC, which exchanged summer jobs between countries for students of economics and commerce. My summer job happened to be in Spain.

The year was 1963 and the Caudillo was still very much in power. In fact, the major avenue in Barcelona known as the Diagonal had been rebaptized the Avenida Francisco Franco during his lifetime. The student who greeted me was eager to point out that Franco would be visiting the city the next day and that the Mercedes in which he would be travelling had been a gift from Adolf Hitler. Something to warm my heart!

The summer turned out to be formative in a number of ways. I shared digs with AIESEC students from Sweden and the Netherlands, became good friends with a French as well as an Italian student, met Spanish students at the student restaurant where I ate, explored the Ramblas and its environs, and felt a growing affinity for Europe. This encounter would not be my last with a city and a country that I would have reason to revisit on more than one occasion, given my future interest in multinational states.

One particular memory comes back to me from that summer. On Saturdays, I would often walk to a park, about 15 to 20 minutes from the apartment where I was staying, and read on a mosaic-decorated bench, looking out towards the Sagrada Familia and the Mediterranean below. There were very few people in the park at the time. If anything, it had a deserted feel to it. Years later, when I returned to Barcelona, I discovered that the park in question was the Park Güell, one of Gaudí's famous creations. Only now it was swarming with tourists and had become a Disney-style attraction.

Barcelona has retained a special place in my heart, in part I think because I associate it with my having been eighteen years old during that summer, the world still waiting to unfold. But it was in another European city that I would find my intellectual bearings and eventually come to spend four seminal years of my life, twice as a student, once on a sabbatical, and once more, this time as a visiting professor — Paris.

I can still remember arriving in Paris in the early morning hours with a few fellow students I had met on the ship on which we had sailed from New York to Le Havre in September 1965. (One could still travel by ship in those years and it had been a student-chartered one to boot!) With my fellowship from McGill, I was free to audit courses pretty much as I chose, some at the Institut d'études politiques (Sciences Po), but others at the Sorbonne or at the graduate faculty known as the École pratique des hautes études. The strongest single memory I have of the courses and seminars I attended that year is of the inaugural lecture by Georges Gurvitch, an eminent sociologist of Russian origin who held a chair at the Sorbonne. (Raymond Aron held the other sociology chair.) The course was supposed to be on twentieth-century sociology, and Gurvitch began: "There is nothing of value in twentieth-century sociology."

I could not believe my ears, nor imagine for a moment a professor at a Canadian university, regardless of discipline, daring to start off on such a note. Gurvitch, like Goethe's Mephistopheles, was "a spirit who denied," although it turned out that there were in fact some things to be learned from twentieth-century sociology — be it the character of power elites, the changing nature of capital and labour, ethnicity and national identities, and much besides. Tragically, Gurvitch died in the middle of my first year in Paris, 1965–66, but I have never forgotten his mordant opening lecture.

Paris was not only about courses and seminars. It was also about films, theatre, concerts, museums, student restaurants, and cafés where one could sit with one's friends opining about the state of the world. There was *Le Monde* to be read assiduously, a newspaper then in its hey-day, with a level of commentary and analysis quite unlike anything one could encounter in Canada. There were the heated political debates. And there were opportunities to travel elsewhere in Europe — to Italy, to England, to Freiburg to visit with a German girl I had befriended on the boat over, to the Soviet Union during the Christmas holidays, and in the summer, to Scandinavia for a trip with my brother, his wife and infant son, then to Greece for a short spell, and finally to Israel.

What did I retain from that first year in Europe? Perhaps most of all a sense of awe at the historical depth of European civilization, the sophistication of its long-established universities, the beauty of some of its cities, all this in contrast with the newness, but also the relative blandness, of the North American cityscapes and universities that I knew. I was certain I would be returning to Europe again.

The next opportunity came in 1969–70, when I received a Canada Council (now SSHRC) fellowship to undertake PhD research in Europe. I returned to Paris, this time living in the Canadian student residence at the Cité universitaire on the south side of the city. Once more I could immerse myself in the cornucopia of academic and cultural treasures the city had to offer, follow the heated political discussions on the French left in the aftermath of the May 1968 events, and spend hours at the Bibliothèque nationale or using the libraries at Sciences Po or the Maison des sciences de l'homme to further my research.

The most important event for me that year was personal. I was to meet my future spouse at the Maison des étudiants canadiens, a Greek student of psychology, Andromaque, in English, Andromache or Mahie for short. We held similar political views which helped cement our relationship, but Eros, as one discovers, follows its own agenda, and by that spring, after a trip together to the Loire, we were fairly smitten with each other. I visited with her in

Greece that summer, and it was clear that our future would be together. We married the following year, 1971, when she came to join me in Vancouver where I had just begun to teach in the Political Science department at UBC.

One of the consequences of marrying into the Greek world was that Greece would eventually become a second home. We spent many a summer, especially after our two sons, Amos and Jonah, were born, journeying back and forth to Volos, the city in Thessaly that Mahie was from, visiting with her mother, brother and future sister-in-law, and in one of the villages on nearby Mount Pelion, where there was a house that had belonged to her grandmother. The village, Tsagarada, had a texture to it unlike anything I had ever encountered before, opening the door to new stimuli and impressions. (I'll have a little more to say about the Greek chapter of my life in the next section.)

Let me return instead to the longer-term impact of my years in Europe. In 1977–78, I had my first sabbatical and as a family we decided to return to Paris. My wife was doing her MA in psychology, our two sons were in kindergarten and daycare respectively, and I spent a fair amount of my time working on a theme which was very much in the air, theories of the state. This had been at the centre of a major dispute on the left between the British Marxist, Ralph Miliband (father of a future leader of the British Labour Party), and a Greco-French Marxist, Nicos Poulantzas. The details of their altercation revolved around the degree of autonomy that the state in capitalist society had vis-à-vis the dominant capitalist class.

I have no interest in revisiting this debate, but I mention it for the following reason. It was precisely at this point that I began to question my faith in Marxist analysis, which had coloured a fair amount of new left thinking in the West, in providing an adequate explanation of political and cultural phenomena. It seemed to me that questions of legitimacy, sovereignty, political leadership and the like could not be reduced in some simplistic fashion to relations of production or of class.

War, in particular, which has so often been the catalyst for major changes in the role of the state in the twentieth century, reinforced the autonomy of the political from purely economic forces. An appeal to national sentiment in crisis conditions can transcend class lines and speak to sentiments of the heart quite at odds with purely material interests. I was in the process of shedding my second orthodoxy, having lost my first, religion, at the age of sixteen.

In my journal, I find the following entry for March 1980: "The bond that snapped in Paris two years ago when I lost my 'faith' in Marxism has much deeper implications than I then realized. I lost my faith in a whole manner of viewing human history, paralleling the theological crisis of my adolescent years. In its stead, the only viable theory I can advance is the time-tested Greek cyclical view of rise and fall and of the contingency of history, politics, and human affairs." I was regaining my intellectual freedom, so to speak, and could feel an iconoclastic stirring in my heart.

As for my own approach to the modern state, the eventual upshot would be a book, *The Masks of Proteus: Canadian Reflections on the State*, published by McGill-Queen's University Press. The book combined elements of political theory and political economy in seeking to map, in a broadly comparative perspective, features of both the Canadian state and of the state *tout court*. It would go on to win a major academic prize for the best book published in the social sciences in Canada in 1990–91.

I was far from finished with Europe or Paris, following my sabbatical year. There were conferences, workshops and congresses to attend in the 1980s and 1990s and I continued to track French intellectual debates. But the times had changed, and the grand theories which had so impressed me in my younger years no longer carried the same weight. The Cartesian clarity of an earlier French discourse was increasingly giving way to the mumbo-jumbo of post-modernism, the new rage in French academic circles, with its complex syntax and incomprehensible prose. By comparison, the empiricism of the Anglo-American tradition, while not without its own limitations, struck me as more illuminating.

Something else began to draw my attention as the years went by, the expansion and evolution of the European Union. It seemed to me that the continent which had given birth to the concept of nationalism and had seen some of the most horrible wars fought in its name was in the process of changing its stripes. True, the Balkans were an unmitigated disaster in the aftermath of the breakup of Yugoslavia. But France and Germany, the old mortal enemies, were at peace with one another, and even Great Britain, for long an island onto itself, had for the moment cast its lot with the continent. Could the European Union prove the harbinger of a new cosmopolitan ethos, setting an example for other regional ensembles, in North America, South America, Southeast Asia, and beyond?

This was still very much in my mind when I returned to Paris for one final year, 2002–3. The Canadian government, when Jean Chrétien was prime minister, had endowed a chair in Canadian Studies at the Sorbonne, and I was its third recipient. My teaching load was light, but I had the opportunity to give seminar presentations at a number of French and European universities during that year and more importantly to begin to reflect on the European-Canadian relationship.

The year also happened to be a dramatic one in international affairs, with a steady drum-beat of war out of Washington preparing the way for the invasion of Iraq. Huge demonstrations in the major cities of the world could not prevent it, but I was struck by how both France and Germany, unlike the United Kingdom, had stood their ground in opposition. And I was proud to see that my own country, not known for standing up to the United States on a major issue of foreign policy, had wisely chosen to stay out of the conflict.

Did that mean that we were more European in some ways than I might have supposed? Was there some deeper instinct at work drawing Canada closer to the old continent, the one from which the overwhelming majority of Canadians had originated? The idea that was to grow into a book-length essay *The European Roots of Canadian Identity* published in 2005 had been born. I will say a little more about this, when I turn to the question of Canadian identity a little later on.

What I did not anticipate, however, was how quickly the worm would turn and the European Union find itself in an existential crisis where its very survival was at stake. True, the international financial crisis of 2008 had major consequences everywhere, and rates of growth in various European countries declined. But this was more palpable in countries of the south like Portugal, Spain, Italy, or Greece, than in Germany or Scandinavia. Suddenly the possibility of a country like Greece being forced to exit the Eurozone was very much on the agenda. And if that wasn't enough, a major inflow of migrants, both from Africa and from the Middle East, began to threaten the borders of Europe, overwhelming the Mediterranean countries on the front line.

Back in February 1995, *Le Monde* had published an article with the following thesis: "The elite have their head in a global world. The population keeps theirs in the national territory." That has turned out to be terribly prophetic. We have seen the United Kingdom leaving the E.U. in the aftermath of the Brexit referendum and the December 2019 election, the refusal of the countries of Eastern Europe to accept even a token number of the refugees/ migrants who have come to the continent, and populist, anti-E.U. parties making major strides, even in Germany. So whither Europe is very much the question of the hour.

I can't claim to have the answer. But I would not be the only one to see in the fatal weakening of the European project a serious setback to those who, having survived two world wars, hoped to construct a different kind of future. And in a world where China is flexing its muscles, where Russia has reverted to an authoritarian mould deeply implanted in its history, and where the United States has a rogue Roman emperor at its helm, a weakened Europe is not in Canada's interest. Our political and social values are more often aligned with those of Western and Northern Europe than with those of the United States, and for economic reasons as well we need effective counterparts to the American colossus.

Let me conclude this section with reflections that have come to me at different moments in my European sojourns. The first was when I was spending a month in Brussels in February 2000, and found myself one Sunday afternoon visiting the battlefield of Waterloo some 30 kilometres south of the city. The sun was in the sky — a bit of a rarity for that time of the year — the fields stretching on and on — here where the French had been encamped, there the British, there the Prussians, there the Russians. With the defeat of Napoleon, a page had been turned in modern European history. What struck me was that almost two centuries had elapsed since this celebrated battle, at least seven or eight generations now separating the living from the dead, and that like other battles of yore — the Thirty Years' War, Poitiers, Actium, Thermopylae — this one was entering the mythic realm. *Les mornes plaines de Waterloo*, as Victor Hugo had called them in a famous poem, were too far distant from us now to matter, as they had for those still alive in the century after the battle. Slowly but surely historical time was displacing all that had come before it.

A second reflection, also inspired by war, came to me when, in the company of my younger son, we were visiting the battlefields of Normandy in 1994, fifty years after the Allied landing. At Bény-sur-Mer there is a Canadian military cemetery, with grave after grave of Canadian soldiers who had died in the battle to liberate Europe from its Nazi scourge. I don't think I have ever felt more Canadian in my life — be it in the foothills of the Rockies, at Tofino overlooking the surf of the Pacific, by Lake Ontario, or in the rolling hills of Quebec's Eastern Townships — as in this tiny piece of Canada set in the pastoral French countryside. It reminded me just how intimately the destinies of Canada and Europe, both for good and ill, have been linked.

A third reflection came to me in Augsburg, which I was visiting in December 2005, for a small Canadian Studies gathering. The Advent market was in full swing in the crisp winter air, but for me, most of all, there was a sense of history. This was where the Romans had built an important encampment named after the first Roman emperor, Augustus, where Luther had defended his still heretical views at the beginning of the Reformation, where Holbein had painted, where Friedrich List in the nineteenth century had developed his views on the importance of a national economy, where Bertolt Brecht, Germany's most important modern playwright, had been born. And I couldn't help contrasting, perhaps unfairly, Augsburg, where the presence of history is overwhelming, with Vancouver, which seemingly lives only for the present.

A final reflection comes from the closing months of our stay in Paris in 1977–78. A journal entry from that period reads: "Coming home on the late Metro from an event-filled day, smell of Paris after the rains, incredibly nostalgic about this city from which I will shortly take my leave. It is surprising how deeply attached I have grown, how many things from street scenes to cafés to the library at the Maison des sciences de l'homme to the bookstores to the cinemas I'll be missing once I have returned to my West Coast home."

My years in Europe had profoundly shaped my intellectual development. In more ways than I could first fathom, they helped set a standard for academic scholarship, cultural openness, and political engagement that would serve me well.

CHAPTER 5

The Muse

I WILL BEGIN WITH a passage from the poem by the German Romantic, Friedrich Hölderlin, entitled "Rousseau":

For those who yearn a sign is enough
and ever since the ancients
signs are the words of the gods.

Why does one write? From where does the impulse come? I have sometimes asked myself these questions and have never answered them to my satisfaction. What I do know is that I began to scribble poetry in my adolescence, even self-publishing a small collection at the ripe old age of sixteen, that I stopped writing during my university years and that I returned to poetry once again when Greece entered my life in a definitive way.

My high school teacher at Herzliah High for both English and History was Irving Layton, a well-known Canadian poet and a mentor to one who would eventually become far better known, Leonard Cohen. In our English classes we were challenged to come up with the hidden meaning of poems like Keats' "Ode to a Nightingale," and threatened with the dire fate of becoming test-tube washers in the Protestant schools if we failed to take our studies seriously. This must have rubbed off on me, but the fact remains that, with one exception, Seymour Mayne, my fellow classmates did not go on to write poetry.

I read widely, including poets like Catullus, Virgil, Dante, Whitman, and Rilke, but it was not obvious that I would ever attempt, however falteringly, to follow in their footsteps. My first collection, *Between Two Holocausts*, was juvenilia of the worst sort — I was no budding Rimbaud about to burst onto the scene! By the age of seventeen, when I had enrolled at McGill, my interests lay far more with politics, economics, or history than with poetry.

I made the right academic moves, completing an Honours degree in Political Science and Economics, going on to do graduate work at McGill, in Paris, and in Toronto, acquiring some useful work experience along the way — a summer position in Canada's External Affairs department in 1965, the CBC in 1967–68 — and eventually beginning what turned into a long and fulfilling university career at the University of British Columbia. Occasionally in those years I might remember my lost muse, but with no illusions that our paths would cross again. Even Paris, so often a stimulus to writers from afar, did little for me in this regard.

And then came Greece. My Greece was not the Hydra of Leonard Cohen, nor the islands that Irving Layton would frequent in his heyday. Volos, my wife's birthplace, was a provincial city in Thessaly with no great claims to fame, at least not in modern times.

But in antiquity, Iolkos, as it was then called, was the point of departure for Jason and the Argonauts in their quest for the Golden Fleece. Moreover, nearby Mount Pelion, where as a family we came to spend part of our summer holidays in the village of Tsagarada, had been the legendary home of the Centaurs, where the Olympian gods had celebrated the marriage of Peleus and Thetis to the accompaniment of the muses, and where the offspring of that union, Achilles, had been raised by the centaur Chiron.

I knew enough by way of Greek mythology for this to begin to move me in strange and unpredictable ways. Little by little, with each visit, I began to scribble again: poems inspired by the landscape of Pelion with its stony mule trails, chestnut trees and running water; by the lives of the inhabitants of Tsagarada, the day-to-day tasks of caring for their crops and their animals, the petty disputes, the gossip, the feast days with their church bells and their evening revelry; by the tales of fortunes made and lost in faraway Pergamon or Egypt. Then there was the sun rising out of the Aegean far below the mountain in the early morning hours. And the seeming presence of the very muses the ancients had evoked.

Writing can be a lonely pursuit. But I felt anything but alone as I surrounded myself in our village house with the poetry of Cavafy, Seferis, or Hölderlin, that great admirer of classical Greece, and with my little library of the Greek tragedians, which I could dip into as the spirit moved me. My writing was neither forced nor driven by the instrumental constraints of an academic text or a newspaper deadline. It seemed to come from some untapped inner source, as though what I was about to put onto paper with my pen (this was still the pre-computer age) had been waiting all along for me to record.

In a 1983 journal entry, I observe: "How right it was to come to Greece. My spirit finds fulfillment in the austerity of the Tsagarada house's four walls, in the continuous presence of the sun, even on cold winter days, in the clear fresco of Pelion I see before me every day. I can fantasize happily about all sorts of things from politics to poetry to nature in its stark simplicity and take more comfort from my writing here than I could ever do elsewhere."

In a subsequent entry written years later, I note: "My moments with the muse, that strange but recurring pattern of poetry writing that has been my wont ever since the 1970s — and in an earlier iteration in the 1950s — for there is an element of redemption associated with these creative moments, that feeling of being touched by a power that stands outside the ordinary course of events. It provides a high point for the life of the mind, an image of promised lands that one only rarely enters."

I consider myself very fortunate to have found in poetry an out-let for my inner thoughts. Or to turn it around, for the muse to have found in me a scribe. For there are times on completing a poem that one is quite overwhelmed by where the impulse and the lines may have come from — they seem to have been dictated by an unseen voice. For me, Volos, and more particularly Pelion, were the home of this unseen voice.

As I was to discover in the years that followed, my muse was no longer confined to Greece. Increasingly in my travels, to Argentina or Japan or India or Spain or Mexico or Paris or Central Europe, I would find myself scribbling in my notebook. A little less frequently in Vancouver, I must confess, and usually with less success. Perhaps my home turf was too familiar a terrain, lacking the appropriate estrangement effect.

In the late 1970s and 1980s, I published several collections of my Greek-inspired poetry, *Poems of Pelion*, *Poems for Andromache*, and in collaboration with a good friend, Ron Walkey, who supplied the drawings, *The Centaur's Mountain*. Nothing to set the world on fire, to be sure, but ample proof that what I had first experienced in my youth had not been a flash in the pan.

Fate, however, that old Greek nemesis, had other things in store for our family. My wife, who had savoured the opportunities to return to her native land, developed a series of chronic illnesses after 2003, and could no longer make the long trip. Nor could I in good conscience, as her caregiver, go gallivanting off alone to Greece or Pelion. Confined to Vancouver for the large part, and having to accompany her through various stages of her long ordeal, I realized that my muse would have to be brought to Vancouver, if I were to continue writing in the poetic vein.

Slowly I began to feel her presence as I walked the trails of Pacific Spirit Park near UBC, or the Seawall near Stanley Park, reacted to a book or film that had impressed me or to the dreary toll of crises and wars in faraway places. By 2015, there was more than enough material for a new collection, *Footsteps of the Past*, published that year by Ronsdale, a Vancouver press. One of the sections of the book dealt with Vancouver, a sure sign that my muse had also found a home here, another section with the infirmity that had become my wife's unhappy lot.

Things, alas, did not improve in that regard. On the contrary, by spring 2016 my wife, her mobility impaired, found herself in hospital for a lengthy period, followed by several months in a full-care facility, only to succumb to her accumulated maladies that fall. My one consolation through her Calvary was the muse, providing an outlet for the sorrow that had become both hers and mine.

Death has its own cruel logic, much like the mourning which follows. I knew that I would now be free to return to Greece, for the first time in fourteen years, bittersweet as the experience would inevitably prove. And that would indeed be the case, both in Volos, in my wife's parental house which still stood much as it had been before, and on Pelion, in Tsagarada where we had spent so many summers *en famille*, and in a cove at the bottom of the mountain, Damouchari, where an old storehouse that had been in my wife's family for generations had been lovingly fixed up by Jonah, our younger son, and my wife's sister-in-law, Sophia.

Chiron the centaur had been known as a healing centaur, and the explanation for this became crystal clear for me in Pelion in the spring of 2017. The mountain was alive with herbs and flowers, many aromatic and therapeutic, and their combination, along with the murmuring sound of the sea below the house in Damouchari and the majestic olive grove behind it began to work their magic. My muse had been waiting to greet me, wondering where I had been all these years. And I could take comfort in our renewed contact.

I published a new collection of poetry with Ronsdale in 2018 called *Passageways* and the final section deals with death and bereavement. But the book also includes selections on other themes, including poems on the Greeks and Hebrews, some of which I had written on Pelion many decades before. I realized then that the poet in me had really come home the previous spring and summer in Damouchari and that I would be coming back to it on a regular basis. Partly as a writer's retreat, to be sure, but equally for the healing spell that Pelion and its muse continue to cast whenever I return.

Some forty years ago, during one of our family's summer stays on Pelion, I penned a poem which I reproduce here by way of a conclusion. As I've come to understand, my desire to write poetry was not born yesterday and its pursuit has provided one of the major underpinnings of my life.

YOU WERE GOING TO BE A WRITER

How did that idea,
hatched in the turbulent, testosterone-charged years
of your adolescence
really take root?
You yearned for pathways to expression,
scribbling what bits you could
in free-form verse and cryptic stories
destined for the drawer.
Yet the urge was there
and through the years,
unknown and unacknowledged,
you have struggled to redeem
what back then seemed an idle promise.

CHAPTER 6

Democracy and its Discontents

IN THE BASEMENT of the Louvre, not much frequented by the swarm of tourists eager to clap their eyes on the *Mona Lisa*, is a series of rooms with Greek antiquities. On one of my visits to the museum, I found myself face to face with a large marble slab originating in fifth century BC Athens. With my faltering knowledge of Greek, I made out the first key words: "The boule (Council) and the Athenian demos have decreed." I felt a thrill, unlike anything I had experienced when I had walked in the shadow of the Parthenon by the Pnyx, where the Athenian assembly had met in the era of Athenian democracy. Here in front of me, in the form of a decree issued by the council and assembly of the Athenian city-state, was testimony to the operation of the first known form of democracy, the one which originated with Cleisthenes in 508 BC and lasted for roughly two centuries until its eclipse in 322 BC.

Much has been written about Athenian democracy, some in praise, e.g. Pericles' famous Funeral Oration reproduced in Thucydides' *History of the Peloponnesian War*, some in bitter condemnation, as in Plato's *Republic*. What we do know is that Athens practised a form of direct democracy, that every citizen had the right to attend meetings of the assembly — held every ten days — where the crucial decisions regarding the city-state were taken, and that in the course of their lives citizens would probably have also served on the council, the executive authority of the city-state. They would not have been elected to the council, but chosen to serve on it for one year on a rotating basis, their names drawn from the registry of their local district (or *deme*). As Aristotle described Athenian-style democracy in his *Politics*, it was based on the principle of ruling and being ruled in turn.

Athenian democracy, to be sure, had serious limitations when compared with the representative version we have today. Its citizenship was limited to males, twenty years of age or older, with parents who were Athenians themselves. Women, foreigners, and slaves were excluded by definition. Moreover, the size and scale of the Athenian city-state, including its interior and coastal peripheries, was picayune when compared to the size and population of most modern nation-states. So even if one aspired to reproduce some variant of its direct democracy today with the more universal basis of citizenship we now have, this would be a near impossibility. One cannot imagine citizens of contemporary liberal democracies, some of whom find voting every four or five years too onerous a task, engaging in the type of ongoing political activity which Athenian democracy would have required. Nor can one see the model easily extended to a large-scale nation-state.

Before I turn to the representative (or indirect) form of democracy that prevails today and say something about the challenges it faces, I need to emphasize something else. Democracy, deriving from the Greek words *demos* (people) and *kratos* (rule), went into decline for over 2,000 years, following the eclipse of the Greek city-state model. Rome, in its classically republican phase, had an element of popular input, but was an aristocratic republic. For millennia, the most common form of political rule, be it in Europe, Asia, Africa or Meso-America, was kingship or empire.

The revival of democracy in the modern era was something of a miracle. It did not come easily or overnight. While representative institutions like parliaments, Estates General, or Diets can be traced back to the Middle Ages, their members were drawn from the nobility, the clergy, or from relatively wealthy landowners or burghers. There was no question of extending the suffrage to the lower classes, as they would have been called, until the era of the French Revolution and well beyond. Only in the American colonies and in the aftermath of the American Revolution did something resembling universal adult white male suffrage make its first appearance.

The main reason the ruling upper classes throughout Europe and even in America were so fearful of democracy was because of the potential threat both to property and acquired status that an emancipated lower class might pose. With democracy, its critics claimed, would come tyranny of the majority and despotism worse than that of abusive monarchs. Before it could be adopted, democracy would have to be constrained through appropriate safeguards.

Hence the numerous checks and balances introduced into the American Constitution, the retention of unelected Upper Houses in European states that had representative institutions, the continued prevalence of hereditary monarchs — many with real power — in most of these, and the slow, incremental extension of the vote to the lower classes. (Women would have to wait until the twentieth century in most countries with representative institutions to acquire the vote.) Another way of saying this is that liberalism, with its notion of individual rights and limits to government, came first and democracy second. And it was not until well into the twentieth century that the term liberal democracy came to be equated with the system of representative government prevailing in most Western states.

There is nothing necessarily wrong with the concept of liberal democracy, to the degree that it provides for such things as individual rights, freedom of the press, and the rule of law along with popular input into government through periodic, fairly run elections and freely competing political parties.

The liberal element and the democratic can, however, sometimes be at odds, and it is not always clear which will win out. We have seen rearguard judiciaries blocking the actions of popularly elected governments (the American Supreme Court at the time of the New Deal comes to mind) and popularly elected governments or rulers running roughshod over the rights of their opponents (contemporary Poland, Hungary, Turkey, and Venezuela come to mind).

The challenges to democracy in its modern guise do not begin or end here. Students of the twentieth century know all too well that democracies can fail in the aftermath of wars or in periods of economic crisis: Mussolini's March on Rome in 1922 or Hitler's accession to power in 1933. They can also fail when recalcitrant militaries turn against what they see as hostile civilian regimes: Spain 1936, Brazil 1964, Chile 1973. And also that revolutions which promise to be emancipatory can quickly become dictatorial: Russia 1917, China 1949. Or that the conditions for democratic transformation may simply not exist in countries that have never known anything but strong-man rule: Libya, Egypt, Syria in the aftermath of the so-called Arab Spring. The triumphalism that led writers like Francis Fukuyama after the fall of the Berlin Wall to assume that liberal democracy would prove the only remaining game in town has quickly turned to dust.

Why might this be so? For starters I would suggest we return for a moment to my earlier observation, namely that one-person rule has been the default line for governance through much of recorded human history. It may offend the democratic sensitivities of those of us who live in reasonably democratic states, but for masses of people throughout the world who have never known viable democratic institutions, these may have little appeal.

What they may find attractive in the Western models conveyed through television, film, or advertising is their high level of affluence, not necessarily their cultural or political underpinnings. Some may still be living in what the German sociologist Max Weber once described as the world of eternal yesterday — radical Islamism is a good example of that. Others may be happy to emulate the economic lifestyle of their counterparts in the West — contemporary China comes to mind — while leaving governance to an all-knowing and ruthlessly controlling party-state. Still others, Central European states like Poland and Hungary now that the Iron Curtain is gone, seem to have reverted to the pre-World War II style of authoritarianism they had known then. And Putin's Russia, not without its modern-day characteristics, has more than passing similarities with the Russia of the Czars and the Commissars. *Plus ça change, plus c'est la même chose.*

But even in the contemporary West, all is not well with democratic institutions and practices. The election of a Donald Trump, the loser in the 2016 presidential election by 3 million votes, because of the arcane workings of an Electoral College devised in the eighteenth century, raises serious questions about whether majority rule applies in the United States. There are similar problems with the first-past-the-post system common to Westminster-style liberal democracies like Canada, where a winning party with under 40 percent of the vote can secure a majority of the seats in Parliament. And then there is the ever-present factor of apathy, the fact that large numbers of electors may not even bother to vote in national, regional, or local elections, that they feel alienated or disempowered from the political system.

Here too there may be a tendency to look for a strong leader, a populist who can point to enemies within and without, and promise the moon and the stars to his followers. We see this in the United States, the supposed shining city on the hill, with a president in office who has open contempt for his opponents, for a critical press, for democratic practices, and purveys all this to his base. The degree of polarization in American society today is intense, threatening the underlying fabric of its institutions. There is evidence of similar polarization in a number of European countries, not to mention Erdogan's dictatorial Turkey or Jair Bolsonaro's Brazil.

Democracy assumes the ability of citizens to differ — as James Madison observed in *The Federalist Papers*, if men were angels they would not need government. But democracy also requires a minimum of shared values, of civility between opponents, and some agreement about the accepted rules of the game. It requires dialogue and discourse to alleviate our more atavistic instincts. And hardest of all, it requires a *demos*, a people — to go back to the original Greek roots of the term — that itself takes democracy, for all its limitations, seriously.

It is by no means certain that democracy, in its liberal democratic guise, will win out against the authoritarian models we see increasingly on display around the world. Nor is it an atrophied model of democracy that can ultimately carry the day. The direct version practised by the Greeks may not be on the agenda. But a more engaged citizenry would certainly help.

What might this entail? One factor would be a greater willingness to join civic organizations that seek to address vital public concerns, be they regarding education, health, the environment, or the community at large. This need not involve a massive commitment of time and energy on the part of their members, merely some willingness to place public interests ahead of purely private ones.

By the same standard, one needs to see some rethinking of the priorities we may have as individual citizens. It is well and good to expect our schools to help train the citizens of the future. But to what extent do the adult citizens of today value the institutions which we currently have and pay attention to the use — or abuse — which those who hold high office make of their power? A major reason for the corrosion in trust that many Western polities have experienced is the perception of significant corruption, both in public institutions and in the powerful private ones which sustain them.

The leaks by major media organizations of documents like the Panama Papers, for example, showed a degree of tax evasion by the top 1–5 percent that beggars the imagination. Yet what has been done by tax authorities to sanction the offenders?

The trail of corruption surrounding the long governing Partido Popular in Spain or members of the country's monarchy had been known for years. But the judiciary, so quick to stomp on would-be separatist politicians in Catalonia, proved positively tortoise-like in its willingness to address these.

The level of corruption in Brazil by its dominant political parties has brought the country to its present impasse with an authoritarian-inclined president now in command. Cynicism can be a dangerous force in democratic societies, much more so than in authoritarian ones. To counteract this cynicism becomes an imperative obligation of engaged citizens.

There is no gainsaying the fact that many other factors can contribute to a malaise with respect to democratic institutions. The fact, for example, that we live in a globalizing age where many of the tools previously at the disposal of national governments have been blunted complicates the picture. It is much harder to have a sense of democratic efficacy when it comes to transnational organizations than to national or sub-national ones. In that sense, the Athenians had a significant advantage over us. But there are ways, through non-governmental international organizations, for example, or sustained pressure on various national governments to attempt to right the balance.

Divisions on key issues — levels of immigration, the balance between environmental and economic interests, the virtue of continued membership in major transnational organizations like the European Union — are not about to vanish, just as divisions were a fact of life in the operation of the ancient city-state. Again, what is important is to prevent divisions from becoming so acute that they fracture shared citizenship beyond repair.

The *demos* may at times be a hard taskmaster, even an unjust one, but when one thinks of the alternatives — aristocratic or oligarchical regimes limited to rule by the few; imperial regimes with their subject populations; authoritarian and totalitarian regimes with their innumerable victims; theocratic ones with their imposed religious codes — the political system we call democracy first invented by the Greeks merits our continuing support.

In the spring of 2018, during a stay in Greece, I revisited Sounion some 75 kilometres from Athens, site of a temple to Poseidon dating from the fifth century BC with a commanding view of the Aegean. When I had first visited it many years before, it had been possible to wander freely amidst its seventeen extant columns. Now one could only walk around their fenced-in perimeter. Still, they were an impressive reminder of the architectural prowess of the ancients.

Something else struck my eye this time around that I had not noticed during that earlier visit. An explanatory notice about the site mentioned that Sounion had been a *deme* or district in one of coastal divisions that had characterized Athenian democracy. And much like in the Louvre, when I had found myself face to face with a decree from the classical era, I had a sense of direct connectedness with the past.

The past does not need to be mythologized. A face-to-face community like that which characterized the Athenian city-state was no guarantee that citizens would place the public good above their private needs. Nor that divisions between the city proper and the outlying periphery, or between those with wealth and those with none, would not exist. Nor that citizens meeting in the Assembly might not fall prey to the appeal of demagogues, something which Thucydides recorded on several occasions in his *History*.

But the ancient model, with which I felt myself vicariously in communion on the day I visited Sounion, reminded me that democracy as an ideal can be a galvanizing force. The Athenian model played that role for several centuries in the larger arena of the Greek city-states. The memory of what had once been a real world example of popular sovereignty in action would take on new resonance when notions of the divine right of kings and of aristocratic rule came to be challenged in the modern era.

The history of the past seventy-five years suggests that this may still be true today. As an aspiration, democracy is no longer confined to the Western world, but has acquired a global dimension. Latin America, which has had its share of aristocratic and military rule, has with a few exceptions taken a democratic turn in recent decades. Eastern Europe, for all the imperfections and backsliding one sees there, has made more of a transition to democratic rule than in the past.

Democratic currents have swept through the Arab world, the African continent, parts of the ex-Soviet Union, and large swathes of South and East Asia as well. Not always with success, to be sure. The repression in Tiananmen Square in June 1989 was one telling example, whose consequences can be felt in China to this day. The failure of the Arab Spring, by and large, was another. So too with glasnost and perestroika in the Soviet Union given what Russia has since become.

Nonetheless, it remains the case that an idea whose origins go back some twenty-five hundred years has not lost its lustre. And that given the opportunity, people in their hundreds of thousands, nay millions, will continue to agitate for the right to determine, not only who will rule them, but to have some meaningful say about the ongoing rules of the game and about the consequences this can have for their daily lives.

CHAPTER 7

On Academic Freedom

I HAVE SPENT MOST of my adult life in universities, first as a student, then as a faculty member at the University of British Columbia. When I travelled abroad, I would often gravitate to universities and their libraries. I have enormous esteem for the spirit of free inquiry that universities, at their best, have historically represented and continue to represent. But I also know that such freedoms are never to be taken for granted, and that they have been threatened or denied on multiple occasions.

In medieval and early modern times, the greatest threat to intellectual freedom in Europe would have come from organized religion in the form of the Church. Galileo had to renege on his view on the rotation of the Earth with respect to the sun in order to save his neck. Giordano Bruno, less fortunate, paid the price for his heretical scientific and philosophical views by being burnt at the stake in Rome's Campo de' Fiori in 1600.

Fortunately, science and humanistic inquiry would not stand still, and the Church began to lose its hegemonic power — first in Northern Europe in the aftermath of the Reformation, and then more broadly with the coming of the Enlightenment. By the eighteenth century, there was an extensive network of philosophers, scientists, and others communicating with each other across national lines in what was often referred to as the republic of letters. For a period, some could even count on "enlightened despots" like Frederick the Great of Prussia or Catherine the Great of Russia for patronage and support.

But the state, which was now beginning to come into its own in various European countries, and in due course elsewhere, could prove a harsh taskmaster. While the French Revolution swept away feudal privileges and much besides, it also saw some of the most eminent scientists and *philosophes* of the day, figures like Lavoisier and Condorcet, perish in the Reign of Terror. In the wave of reaction which swept continental Europe in the aftermath of the Napoleonic Wars, there was little place for critical thinking, be it in Metternich's Austria, Nicholas I's Russia, or Frederick Wilhelm IV's Prussia. State censorship ensured that heretical ideas were kept at bay, even as vigilant state officials kept a close eye on university affairs.

The pattern improved somewhat in the second half of the nineteenth century and into the early twentieth. The modern-style university, with its division between disciplines and faculties, with a mandate for serious research, and with a degree of autonomy vis-à-vis the state, made its appearance. Once again, there was something of a republic of letters in the air, with collaboration and interaction between scholars in various fields and with scientific journals and publications that crossed national lines.

The two world wars, however, did much to destroy this. German universities, which had long served as a model for countries like the United States, could not survive the Weimar years intact. Hitler's coming to power spelled the elimination of "non-Aryan" and other so-called "undesirable elements," and the complete subordination of higher education to the Nazi regime. Things were not much better in fascist Italy. At the other end of the political spectrum, there was little room for independent thought in the Soviet Union, especially during the Stalin years, with ideological conformity at a premium. Subsequently, despite the thaw in the Khrushchev years, party control over higher education continued.

I had a vivid experience of this when I attended a World Congress of the International Political Science Association held in Moscow in 1979 during the Brezhnev years. In session after session, regardless of topic, delegates from the Soviet Union or its more faithful East European allies, if they were on a panel, would read carefully screened papers conforming to party line, or proceed to articulate the appropriate party position during the question and answer period. One knew what was coming before a delegate had uttered a word!

The suppression of academic freedom is a sure sign of an authoritarian regime. One saw it, *in extremis*, during the Cultural Revolution in China, when academics accused of deviation from Mao Tse-tung's thought were humiliated, tortured, or killed without remorse. Things have improved in China since, but pity the Chinese academic who would dare evoke Tiananmen Square, inquire into the true state of affairs in Xinjiang or Tibet, or offer even a muted critique of the dominant role played by the Chinese Communist Party and its current leader for life. What goes for China goes for many other countries. Hungary has forced the Central European University financed by George Soros to decamp from

Budapest to Vienna because its broadly liberal values are at odds with those of its governing regime. Under Erdogan, Turkey has purged thousands of academics from its universities and maintains heightened control over those who remain, under the guise of defence of the state. Sisi's Egypt is no bastion of academic freedom. The list could go on and on.

Western countries, where academic freedom has generally been better protected, have also seen significant violations of the principle over the years. The McCarthyite years in the United States were not good ones for scholars accused of sympathy for left-wing causes. In Canada, the Canadian Association of University Teachers has documented numerous examples of university administrations which have acted arbitrarily towards faculty members. And here too there have been provincial governments and premiers like George Drew in Ontario and Maurice Duplessis in Quebec who have not hesitated to attack prominent academics on political grounds or threaten to withhold funding, if universities would not do their bidding.

Still, for the most part, there is now an arm's length relationship between governments and universities in this country and an understanding of the importance of university autonomy. One saw this in 2018 when controversy blew up over the decision of the University of Alberta to award an honorary degree to David Suzuki. With the oil and gas industry in Alberta's oil sands under sustained attack from environmentalists like Suzuki, there were numerous calls, including from two of its own deans, for the university to reverse its decision. To her credit, then-Premier Rachel Notley, while critical of the decision, made it clear that it was for the university, not the government, to determine who should be given such awards.

This incident, however, highlights something else, the increasing importance of corporate donors to the operation of universities and the impact this can have. Pharmaceutical companies, for example, have a high stake in the development of new drugs and will often fund research carried out in universities. But they may not welcome adverse commentaries on the potential safety of their products and may try to ensure that those they fund will toe the appropriate line. In 2000, David Healy, a British research scientist, found his job offer from a health research institute affiliated with the University of Toronto rescinded. He had been a critic of the popular antidepressant Prozac, and the institute in question had received major funding from Eli Lilly, the drug's manufacturer. What goes for pharmaceutical companies can easily apply to other major corporate donors. One thinks of Huawei, with strong ties to the Chinese state, which has been funding a fair amount of computer science research in Canadian universities. Are such relationships without long-term consequences?

Back in 1946, Harold Innis, Canada's pre-eminent economic historian, had argued that "the descent of the university into the marketplace was the lie at the heart of modern society." Little did he know what the future would have in store! As universities have expanded in size and scale, they have become ever more dependent on outside funding, in addition to government subsidies and student fees, to finance their activities. Some of this comes from alumni, but a major source has become the corporate sector.

There will be trade-offs in the process. Major buildings, facilities, or chairs may be named after a particular corporate donor, introducing a strongly commercial element into an institution where it does not really belong. Or a company may be given certain privileges in exchange for its contributions. An example I remember from the period when I was a faculty member on UBC's Board of Governors in the late 1990s was Coca-Cola, which was given a monopoly on the marketing of beverages on the university campus. The details of the arrangement were hushed up by the administration — there were financial benefits flowing to the university — but the heart of the matter was a strictly commercial venture, one of many in which universities now engage.

How well can universities defend principles of academic freedom, when major financial interests may be at stake? How can they ensure that their hiring priorities are not unduly influenced by pressures emanating from the private sector? Formal procedures may be put in place to try ensure the continuing autonomy of researchers and scholars working in a university setting. But informal pressures of all kinds can be applied and the knowledge that funding is coming from a particular corporate or industry source can strongly colour the direction that hiring and research may take. The core commitment of universities to the teaching of the arts and sciences needs to be protected from pressures to succumb to a purely market-driven approach. While professional and vocational training is a legitimate component of any modern-day university, a commitment to critical thinking in the humanities and social sciences and to pure, unfettered research in the natural sciences is what universities need to value above all else.

The major threats to academic freedom have tended to come from outside — religious orthodoxy, state interference, excessive corporate influence. However, threats can also come from within. In recent decades, one has seen battles around which speakers should or should not be allowed onto campuses, about statements made in the classroom that individuals or groups may find offensive, about what some judge to be a hostile or chilly climate in the academy. More often than not, the major proponents of curtailing what should be permitted on campus have tended to situate themselves on the left.

Thinking back to the 1960s for a moment, I recall that the student left was pursuing a very different agenda. The Berkeley Free Speech movement, as its name would suggest, was about ensuring that there would be spaces on campus where freedom of speech in the broadest sense, including opposition to the war in Vietnam, would be permitted. The students in Paris in May 1968 who argued "It is forbidden to forbid" were on a similar wave-length. So what has changed?

The difference lies in the rise of what has come to be called identity politics. Politicization in universities in recent decades has tended to occur around issues such as gender, race, or ethnicity. Proponents of radical agendas linked to these causes have tended to see themselves as victims of a sexist or racist institution and faculty members as complicit beneficiaries in its operation. Academic freedom under these circumstances is seen as little more than a subterfuge for white, male privilege and aggrieved students have every reason to subject it to attack.

Along with members of my department, I had a direct encounter with such thinking back in 1995. About a dozen female graduate students, a number of them women of colour, levelled wholesale charges against what was then a largely male department, accusing it of systemic racism and sexism in its treatment of its female graduate students. The Dean of Graduate Students was sympathetic to their cause and the university administration proceeded to shut down admissions into the department's graduate program and to hire a lawyer, Joan McEwen, to conduct an inquiry into the issues that had been raised.

The inquiry went on for months and ended up costing the university the hefty sum of $250,000. It concluded, often quoting statements by faculty members out of context and anecdotal claims of little merit, that a chilly climate, hostile to female and minority students, had been created in the department and needed to be addressed.

Some months later, with the public row becoming an embarrassment to the administration, the suspension of admissions to the department's graduate program was lifted. A number of the aggrieved students, however, proceeded to take matters to the provincial Human Rights Commission, demanding a significant sum of money and even the retroactive award of their graduate degree as compensation for their supposed victimization. The commission, in due course, rejected their claims, and the university administration a few years later, under a new president, offered the department a formal apology for the unjustified actions that had been taken against it.

In the short term, damage had been done to the department's reputation, though in the long run it has continued to be one of the leading political science departments in the country. Moreover, it has become much more diversified in its faculty, partly in reaction to the events of 1995, but more importantly, as a consequence of the growing diversity by gender, race, and ethnicity of the pool of graduate students across the university system at large from which one can hire new recruits.

As I wrote in my journal dated July 7, 1995: "The troubling part of the McEwen Report and what has followed is the implication that even one's unconscious behaviour is potentially culpable, that white males, for example, merely by being who they are and going about their business in a normal fashion, are carrying the seeds of racism and sexism. Specific words or gestures now become part of a larger pattern of discriminatory behaviour.

"It is enough that members of a designated group perceive themselves to be at the receiving end of discriminatory behaviour for the inquiry to conclude that such behaviour *de facto* exists. And this can outweigh the 99.9 percent of what goes on in the academic world that seemingly has nothing to do with discriminatory interactions of any kind.

"To go from palpable and specific acts of discrimination to vaguely articulated 'feelings' or 'climates' is to cross a line. To imply that it behooves members of a historically privileged majority group to prove that they are, consciously or unconsciously, not engaged in discriminatory behaviour is to render most forms of interaction between members of these two constituencies prickly in the extreme. It is to shift the burden of proof where discrimination is concerned to thoughts, feelings, and unintended consequences.

"It is also to make it very difficult to continue to think of universities as communities of faculty, student and staff or of academic debate and discussion as fairly free and unconstrained. *En garde* seems to be the message of the more militant forms of feminism and anti-racism. In the process, these can only engender a powerful counter-reaction and wreak havoc on the functioning of academic institutions."

The point I want to emphasize is that identity politics can affect the operation of a university, and not necessarily for the better. It has led to attempts to censure a teaching assistant at Wilfred Laurier University who refused to conform to the gender-free speech code of some of her strongly politicized students. Where speech is concerned, one needs to ensure that universities remain arenas where controversial issues can be explored. For example, for a classroom to introduce passages from Hitler's *Mein Kampf* in a discussion of fascism does not constitute advocacy of Hitler's views. The same would be true when dealing in the classroom with some of the anti-Oriental sentiments that pervaded a province like B.C. at the beginning of the twentieth century. To cite them is not the same thing as extolling them.

My position is that universities should provide the maximum space possible for free speech, subject to clear limits in the law, e.g. the advocacy of violence. The proponents of forms of identity politics, much like the proponents of different political causes, should not seek to usurp the freedom the university offers them in order to deny equivalent rights to those with whom they disagree. Nor should they emulate the McCarthyite tactics that were once used to tarnish the reputations of bona fide scholars in the era of the Cold War.

Hannah Arendt, one of the twentieth century's most lucid political theorists, observed in her study on *The Origins of Totalitarianism* that every ideology was potentially capable of veering off in a totalitarian direction. We know what the history of fascism and communism teaches us in this regard. We can see where radical Islamism can lead. But we need to be wary in this regard even of familiar ideologies like conservatism, liberalism, or socialism, not to speak of nationalism, and the same would hold true for newer ones like feminism, anti-racism, or environmentalism. For hard-core adherents of any ideology, much like hard-core adherents of religious orthodoxy, there may be only one truth — *their* truth. And that can lead to the dismissal of any and all criticism and to the attempted suppression of rival points of view.

Academic freedom remains a key principle for universities that cherish free inquiry in the pursuit of knowledge. Faculty, administrators, and students alike need to be extremely vigilant in its defence, all the more so knowing that in many parts of the world such principles are systematically denied.

CHAPTER 8

Revisiting Canadian
Identity

CANADA IS A LUCKY country — immense, splendidly endowed
in natural resources, with a reasonably sized population, a high
standard of living, and a location far from the major war zones and
fault lines of the world. Yet it suffers, or has periodically suffered,
from an identity crisis that has still not been resolved.

To begin with there is the English-French division that pre-
cedes Confederation and that has at times provoked crises that
have threatened to tear the country apart. These would include the
aftermath of the hanging of Louis Riel, the Manitoba and Ontario
School Questions, conscription during the two world wars, and the
challenge of Quebec separatism between 1960 and 1995.

There are significant regional differences that have also under-
mined the country's cohesion: Atlantic Canada with its own internal
divisions; Quebec a province with national aspirations; Ontario,

Canada's dominant province demographically and economically, sometimes seen as lording it over the others; the Prairies divided among three provinces but often at loggerheads with central Canada; B.C. sometimes a region onto itself, sometimes allied with its western neighbours against the east; and the three northern territories, immense in size but minuscule in population.

There are Canada's First Nations, spread over the length and breadth of the country, some living on reserves, the majority in urban conglomerations, some with significant resources at their command, others living in conditions reminiscent of Third World countries. Their political role has become a good deal more important in recent decades with the coming of the Charter and the entrenchment of Indigenous rights through the courts.

To this one can add the multicultural component, once constituted primarily of immigrants and their descendants of south and east European background, but with the removal of geographical and racial barriers in Canada's immigration policy after 1967, increasingly made up of immigrants and their descendants from East Asia, South Asia, and other parts of the world.

These different plates by themselves constitute one important part of the Canadian identity puzzle, but the story does not end here. A second key element resides in the way the country was created in 1867 out of four British North American colonies through an act of the British Parliament and with ongoing links to Great Britain. These were more than symbolic. Until 1931, dominions like Canada were not fully independent in their foreign policy; until 1949, the highest court of appeal in matters of Canadian jurisprudence was the Privy Council in London; until 1952, all the Governors General of Canada had been British citizens; until 1965, the Canadian flag was the Red Ensign, featuring the British Union Jack in one corner; until 1982, amendments to

Canada's constitution needed to go through the British Parliament; and to this day a British monarch remains the country's formal head of state.

The British connection has had positive aspects, to be sure. Britain's status as a great power in the nineteenth century preserved much of future British Columbia from American takeover in 1847–48, the period of American manifest destiny, and the call of "54–40 or fight" where the border between the Oregon territory and British-controlled territory to the north was concerned. (Compare poor Mexico in this regard, which lost half of its territory during that period!) British parliamentary institutions have, on the whole, worked well and provided Canada and its provinces with effective and stable, if at times strong-armed, government, although democratically deficient ones in the absence of some variant of proportional representation. The relations between the two countries, reinforced in wartime even more than in times of peace, have generally been very close, not least in the economic sphere during Canada's first half-century before World War I. But where identity has been concerned, disengaging Canada from its British underpinnings has not always proved straightforward.

A third key element has been Canada's location on the North American continent, side by side with an expansive United States — the dominant global power since 1945. It is never easy playing second fiddle to a larger neighbour. New Zealand has experienced this with respect to Australia, Ireland with respect to Great Britain, Austria with respect to Germany, the Ukraine with respect to Russia. And given the extensive ties that were to develop between Canada and the United States over two centuries — demographic, economic, cultural, military, political — the American connection has often posed challenges to the emergence of a stronger sense of Canadian identity.

Certain features of that identity are easier to summon up than others. Canada's geographical location in the northern part of North America, with a harsh winter climate to boot, was already highlighted in the nineteenth century paintings of Cornelius Krieghoff. Between the two world wars, Canada's most important school of painters, the Group of Seven, found inspiration for their work in the Laurentian Shield, the Great Lakes, and the Rockies.

The physical geography of a country alone, however, does not give it a cultural or political identity. John A. Macdonald, Canada's first prime minister, campaigning in the 1891 election, his last, proudly claimed: "A British subject I was born, a British subject I shall die." But the bloodletting of World War I, with over 60,000 Canadian soldiers killed in battles like Vimy Ridge, left many in Canada conscious of the country's need to affirm its own national identity. And this is what gradually occurred, with Canada's presence at the Paris peace conference in 1919, with its membership in the ill-fated League of Nations, with its increasing diplomatic outreach in the late 1920s, culminating in the Statute of Westminster of 1931 which formalized its independent international status from Great Britain.

More of this was to follow Canada's exemplary contribution to Allied victory in World War II. With Great Britain much weakened in the aftermath of the war and its empire a thing of the past, Canada could loosen its bonds. The Canadian Citizenship Act of 1947 was a major step in this direction, as was the ending of appeals to the Privy Council in 1949, the naming of Canadians as Governors General from 1952 on, the adoption of the Maple Leaf flag in 1965, and the patriation of the Canadian constitution from the United Kingdom in 1982. Only the monarchy continues to remain, sadly in my opinion, as a legacy from our colonial past.

Even as Canada was affirming its national identity vis-à-vis

Great Britain, it was falling more and more under the sway of a quite different empire, the American. By the 1920s, the United States had replaced Britain as the major source of foreign investment in the country. Beginning with the Permanent Joint Board of Defence between Canada and the United States set up in 1940, reinforced by agreements such as NORAD (North American Air Defence Command) of 1957, Canada would be engaged as a junior partner to the United States through the long decades of the Cold War. Canada's foreign policy would rarely deviate from that of its powerful southern neighbour, while ties between the people, no less than the governments, of the two countries were extremely close.

There were, however, misgivings about the consequences all this might have for the country's identity. An early example came with the Massey Royal Commission on the Arts, Letters, and Sciences which in its 1951 report highlighted the importance of fostering a Canadian culture distinct from that of the United States and Canadian universities able to educate Canadian graduate students at home. The establishment of the Canada Council for the Arts in 1957, with its funding for Canadian artists and writers, and the beginning of federal funding of university level research followed as well.

The 1960s, as I suggested in an earlier section, saw an unprecedented wave of Canadian nationalism, partly in reaction to the Vietnam War, partly out of concern for what seemed to be inordinate control by major American corporations over the Canadian economy. The Foreign Investment Review Agency was set up in 1973 to ensure that foreign acquisitions of Canadian companies would be beneficial to the country. In the cultural arena, Canadians began to pay more attention to Canadian literature, popular music, and theatre than before. Canadian universities found themselves under pressure to give precedence to Canadians in their hiring policies. In foreign policy, there was talk of a third way, less dependent on the United States, more open to other parts of the world. Some of this would be reversed from the 1980s on with the coming of the Free Trade Agreement between Canada and the United States in 1988, followed by NAFTA in 1993. Yet Canadian public policies and political culture would prove surprisingly resilient in the decades that followed and the country seems to have less of an inferiority complex vis-à-vis the United States at the moment than in an earlier day. The disaster of the American-initiated Iraqi invasion of 2003, which the Chrétien government had opposed, may have helped. So too the rampant gun culture in the United States which most Canadians abhor. The accession of a petulant bully to the American presidency in 2017 has only reinforced a sense of Canadian distinctiveness, where our underlying civic culture is concerned.

In the course of my academic career, I have had frequent occasion to reflect on the nature of Canadian identity. A fair amount of my research and writing has focused on the relationship between Quebec and the rest of Canada and I can perhaps best sum up my thoughts in this regard with a journal entry from twenty years ago: "Canadian has two different meanings. It is a term of *formal state citizenship*, e.g. the passport one carries when travelling abroad, for most of us living within the country's borders. And it is a term of *nationality or national identity* for the twenty-eight million Canadians outside Quebec and for a certain percentage of Québécois and Indigenous people, but by no means all, who also use it in the second sense. A portion of our national malaise flows from the clash between these two plates and from the terminological ambiguity inherent in the term 'Canadian.'"

To my mind, Canada is not just a federal state in the classical territorial way that the United States or Australia, to think of two comparable cases, are federations. Canada also has some of the characteristics of a multinational federation or state, clearly so where Quebec is concerned, increasingly so as well, when First Nations, Inuit, or Métis enter the picture. This can compound the difficulties of decision-making at the federal level — the Canada Pension Plan of the 1960s with a separate Quebec Pension Plan alongside — and at the provincial/territorial level as well, when Indigenous claims are at stake. One needs to try find agreement across these divides, placing a higher premium on consensus than might have been true otherwise. To quote the winning entry to a CBC *Morningside* competition of the 1990s about Canadian values: "As Canadian as possible under the circumstances."

I have also argued in my book *The European Roots of Canadian Identity* that, in numerous ways, Canada is more of a European-type state than the United States. English-speaking Canadians never experienced the radical break with Great Britain that the American Revolution represented. On the French-Canadian side, *je me souviens* was more than a motto for license plates. It spoke to an ongoing, if at times muted, sentiment for *le vieux pays*, i.e. France, reinforced in recent times by the enhanced role of language, as opposed to religion, in the affirmation of Quebec identity. It also helps explain the emphasis on a shared civic identity that Quebec's recently passed Bill 21, which bars teachers, police officers, and government officials from wearing personal religious symbols, evokes — a mirror reflection of French views in this regard.

As a middle-sized power, Canada's role in global affairs has closely resembled that of the Scandinavian countries or the Netherlands, conscious of the need to mediate international conflicts where possible. Social policies like Medicare bring us much closer to the European norm, and in our historical use of government we have not shared the American disdain for state over market.

Another element one could point to, for English Canada no less than Quebec at present, is a more secular view of society, with hard-line religious fundamentalism of the American sort significantly weaker here. Finally, and perhaps most importantly, Canadians do not have the hubris that has so often marked the American temperament. We are more like Hamlet in this regard, more given to self-doubt — not unlike the Europe of today.

Yet in good dialectical fashion (something of the Hegelian-Marxist approach must have rubbed off on me), I would also acknowledge Canada's profoundly North American character. In what was my final book-length academic contribution, *The Labyrinth of North American Identities*, I sought to explore some of the common features of the three countries, Canada, the United States, and Mexico, that in 1993 teamed up to form NAFTA (now morphed into USMCA).

All three had Indigenous populations before the arrival of the Europeans, which despite their marginalization and, in some cases, even extermination, have left a significant impact down to today. In all three, religion, be it Catholicism or Protestantism, imported from Europe played a crucial foundational role, though it might take syncretic and novel forms on this continent, e.g. the cult of the Virgin of Guadalupe in Mexico, the proliferation of Protestant sects in the United States and to a lesser degree in Canada. Spanish, English, and French as spoken on this continent became more informal than the versions spoken in the respective courts of Europe, more innovative in their need to describe North American fauna, flora, and geography, more open because of immigration or contact with one another to absorbing words from other languages.

All three countries, because of their size, developed as federations, with strong regional identities. Both state and market have played an important role in their development, although the three have diverged from each other with regards to their respective roles. All three have sometimes seen themselves as chosen peoples, the Americans far more so than the other two! And, of course, all three share a stake in the continent they call home, and will continue to do so with or without any ongoing free trade agreement.

Well and good, one might say, but where does this leave Canadian identity? In the summer of 1992, at the height of our constitutional debates, I found myself at Nakoda, in the foothills of the Rockies, as one of 45 participants from across the country and from varying backgrounds debating that very question. And not to my surprise, after a pleasant week in each other's company and some passionate discussions, each of us returned to our respective homes not much more enlightened, I'm sorry to report, than before. And the same would be true, I suspect, for the many other panels and discussions of Canadian identity that have been held since.

What I can offer by way of conclusion to this section are a few thoughts. The three facets I have outlined in this section, the multinational state component, the European component, and the North American, constitute intersecting plates. Each has played an important role in shaping the country, though none to the total exclusion of the other two. I have no reason to believe that this has ceased to be the case, although arguably the Pacific will loom larger in Canada's twenty-first-century destiny than was true in the past.

It might also make sense to consider what would constitute core Canadian values. Here is a short list taken from my book on *The European Roots of Canadian Identity*:

- A sense of living together within a common geographical space in the northern part of North America.
- Evolving political practices based upon representative institutions of a parliamentary kind.

- A European-derived legal and constitutional tradition with added features of our own.
- An understanding of the obligations, and not only the rights and privileges, that come from membership in a free society.
- Welfare state policies entailing a solidarity linked to common citizenship.

I would not claim for a moment that these represent the last word on the subject and that others could not come up with lists of their own. It is one stab at the topic.

I would also pick up on a comment which Stéphane Dion made, back in his days as Minister for Intergovernmental Affairs in the Chrétien government: "Canada is a country which works in practice, but not in theory." This may sound like a cop-out for those seeking greater clarity on the subject, but in some ways it is not, for our fate as Canadians may resemble that of Sisyphus in the Greek legend, condemned to roll a boulder up the hill for all eternity, only to see it roll down again once it has reached the top.

CHAPTER 9

West Coast
Reflections

I MOVED TO VANCOUVER in 1971 to take up a teaching position
at the University of British Columbia. At the time, I thought of this
as a temporary berth — my heart was set on returning to Montreal,
preferably to a francophone university like the Université du Québec
à Montréal. Europe was still lingering in the background, so much
closer to Eastern Canada than to the country's Pacific Coast.

I wasn't cut out to be a good British Columbian. I had too strong
a sense of the past, in a province where only the present and the future seemed to matter. I wasn't a rugged outdoors type, passionate
about skiing in the winter and camping in pristine mountain wilder-
nesses in the summer. I had an intellectual disposition, something
that did not quite fit the typical British Columbian profile. And I
had a tragic sense of life, totally out of sync with my new milieu.

Yet somewhat to my surprise the city and province began to grow on me. It helped that there was a newly elected NDP government headed by Dave Barrett, the province's first, a year after my arrival. That gave me something to identify with (I became and remained a party member for a fairly long stretch of time) as well as something to write about. It also helped that my department was a pleasant and, on the whole, a harmonious one, supportive of scholarship even from a black sheep with a left-wing reputation as I had.

As marriage and children entered the picture, Vancouver began to feel more like home. New friendships were formed, I became a frequent commentator on local and national media, even as provincial politics began to heat up. I particularly remember the year 1983. In a closely fought election, the Social Credit government under Bill Bennett was re-elected and proceeded to introduce a very tough budget that among other measures severely limited the rights of public sector unions, dramatically cut social spending, and eliminated rent controls.

By autumn, a wide-ranging coalition of trade unions and social movements called Operation Solidarity had been formed (the name had been borrowed from the Polish trade union movement of the same name headed by Lech Wałęsa). In addition, a strike in the public sector, to be followed by one in the private sector, was in the cards.

When the strike kicked off in early November, I helped to organize a group of UBC faculty members who decided to respect the picket lines at the university by not holding classes. The Committee of Concerned Academics, as we called ourselves, also organized a trek from the campus to downtown Vancouver to protest the government's actions and took out a full-page ad with hundreds of signatures in the *Vancouver Sun* to oppose threatened cuts to higher education.

In the event, the public sector strike ended after four days, following a hastily convened meeting in Kelowna between Jack Munro, the head of the province's leading private sector union, the IWA, and the premier and his chief advisor. But the mood remained fraught on campus, as universities like UBC struggled to deal with the financial fall-out from the budget. B.C., it turned out, had been the first Canadian province to implement the hard-nosed, neo-conservative policies associated with Margaret Thatcher and Ronald Reagan, and it would not be the last.

My next memorable moment where B.C. politics is concerned came a decade later. This was during the Meech and Charlottetown debates, when constitutional reform dominated the national agenda. I had taken a public position against Meech for the reasons I mentioned earlier — what I saw as the excessive weakening of the federal government.

1991 had seen the election of a second NDP government, this one under Mike Harcourt. I was appointed to an advisory committee of the NDP on constitutional matters. But when the Charlottetown Accord became the provincial party's official position, I found myself the odd man out, opposing it for much the same reason I had opposed the Meech Lake Accord.

In the event, I was much closer to majority sentiment in the province when the October 1992 referendum on Charlottetown was held, with 68 percent of British Columbians voting No. Although the reasons for many British Columbians voting that way were not always the same as mine.

One further round of discussions, this one involving the nine provinces other than Quebec, took place in 1997 around a document known as the Calgary Accord. I mention it, not because it got the constitutional debate back on the rails, but because it resulted in a series of meetings around the province where ordinary citizens could state their views on British Columbia and Canadian

PHILIP RESNICK

unity. With the help of a post-doctoral student, Victor Armony, I was able to process the multiple presentations made on this occasion. The result was a book I published in 2000 entitled *The Politics of Resentment: British Columbia Regionalism and Canadian Unity.* The book sought to explore the nature of regionalism in the B.C. context, contrasting it in the process with the nationalism I had often written about in Quebec. I emphasized the geographical isolation of the province, framed by a sea of mountains and physically far removed from the political centre of the country. Its political leaders going back to the beginning of the twentieth century had often found themselves at loggerheads with the federal government. Nor had B.C. politicians, unlike their counterparts in a province like Alberta, sought to play a leading role in federal affairs. Among the population at large, many newly arrived from other parts of Canada or from overseas, there was a tendency to think of the province as a micro-world unto itself. How the province would have related to the rest of Canada in the event of Quebec separation was very much an open question. Yet there was a deep current of identification with Canada in B.C., just as there had been with Great Britain in an earlier period.

In 2002–3, I found myself back in Paris for a year, as the holder of the chair in Canadian Studies at the Université de Paris III-Sorbonne Nouvelle. A wonderful opportunity, it seemed, for both my wife and me to renew our ties with a city we had cherished for so long. We had found an apartment in the Latin Quarter, cheek by jowl with the Jardin du Luxembourg, as central a location as one could hope for. Yet almost from the moment of our arrival, I felt that something was missing. The street noises, blaring sirens and all, reminded me that we were in the midst of a large, crowded city. The Luxemburg Garden, while a pleasant oasis from its built-up surroundings, was not all that large and lacked the abundant greenery I had grown used to back home.

108

Where were the snow-capped mountains of the North Shore, visible from Spanish Banks or English Bay, opening to the Strait of Georgia and Vancouver Island? I was experiencing an epiphany of sorts, realizing just how much the physical landscape of B.C., its mountains and forests and sea, had become an integral part of my mental space. Finally, after all these years, Vancouver was truly home and I would never again think of it in any other way.

Towards the end of my UBC career, I opted to teach the course on B.C. politics. It was an opportunity for me to pull together my thoughts on the political economy of the province, its colourful, though at times, checkered and intolerant history, its electoral track record, both provincially and federally, its political parties, governmental institutions, key interest groups and social movements. But there was something else I wanted to add to the mix, a framework for thinking about the province in a broader, more comparative manner. This seems like a good way to cap my reflections in this section as well.

I can think of four different perspectives or templates on B.C. The first and most obvious is as a region unto itself, what Jean Barman in her book on the province called *The West beyond the West*. Although B.C. for certain purposes is part of Western Canada, it has seldom fitted into the equation in the same way as the Prairie provinces. It did not have a wheat-based economy, nor the oil reserves which would fuel Alberta's post-war boom. What it did have were important resources of its own — forestry, minerals, a rich fishery, hydro electricity, and perhaps most important of all, a location on the Pacific, giving it direct access to the seaways of the world. It also had unsettled Indigenous land claims, which have come back to haunt it in recent decades. And it has an increasingly diverse ethnic mix, with a larger Asian population, proportionately speaking, than any other province.

A second perspective on B.C. is to see it as part of a putative
region known as Cascadia. This points to important similarities
between B.C. and its two American neighbours, Washington and
Oregon. All three are located in the Pacific Northwest of the continent, have a similar resource base in their past histories, and have
often seen themselves as far-removed from the political centres of
their two countries. But there is more to the story, as Douglas Todd
was to show, through a volume he edited entitled *Cascadia: The
Elusive Utopia*. It turns out that the inhabitants of Cascadia have
the lowest rates of identification with organized religion on the
continent. There may be forms of spirituality in Cascadia, but
much of it is personal or nature-based as opposed to theological in
the traditional sense. Not surprisingly, ecological concerns loom
large here and shape the larger political landscape. One has seen
this recently with the strong opposition in B.C. to the expansion of
the Kinder Morgan pipeline from Alberta to the coast.

Even the governor of Washington has weighed in on the side of
the current B.C. government, sharing concerns about possible oil
spills to the coast. For certain purposes, therefore, the Cascadia
lens can be helpful in understanding B.C. The internal divisions
between interior and metropolitan centres in all three jurisdictions,
B.C., Washington, and Oregon, however, suggest the need for
caution in this regard. For the more socially liberal and pro-envi-
ronmental views one finds in cities like Vancouver, Seattle, and
Portland are not echoed in the resource-based parts of B.C., Washington, and Oregon where conservative and pro-developmental
views predominate.

A third perspective on B.C. is what I would call California
north. B.C. is to the rest of Canada what California has been to the
United States, the westernmost part of the country to which many
have sought to escape, the end of the rainbow where dreams of

remaking oneself can be realized. Of course, the reality can be grimmer than that. One thinks of the druggies and homeless on Vancouver's downtown eastside and of their equivalent in San Francisco's tenderloin district or in Los Angeles' Skid Row. Still, for the majority of its inhabitants, B.C. like California holds promises of a lifestyle that combines work in a pleasant environment with multiple opportunities for physical well-being.

Hollywood has turned parts of British Columbia, the Lower Mainland in particular, into a setting for some of its films, and there is constant traffic up and down the coast of those engaged in high tech and new age activities. But as with Cascadia, a note of caution is in order. California has a population that exceeds that of Canada as a whole, and has assumed a leading role world-wide in the development of new technologies. B.C., by comparison, is a mere follower. There can also be a shallowness to the much-touted West Coast lifestyle. As William Faulkner noted, after a stay in the California of the early 1930s, "its youth were as beautiful as gods and goddesses, but with the minds of infants." Less true today, perhaps, for both California and B.C., but with a grain of truth to it, nonetheless.

A fourth perspective on B.C. is what I would call Asia Pacific. There is something ironic about the recent turn of events, with the emergence of China as a major economic rival to the United States and with the significant rise of immigration, capital flow, and money laundering (one thinks of the housing market) from East Asia and to a lesser degree South Asia to B.C.

At the turn of the twentieth century, after all, B.C. was a province with a strongly anti-Asian culture, where there were riots in Chinese and Japanese neighbourhoods in 1907 and a mass turnout in 1914 to prevent the unloading of the *Komagata Maru* with its would-be migrants from the Punjab. During World War II,

PHILIP RESNICK

Japanese Canadians bore the brunt of wartime hysteria, expelled en masse from the West Coast in the aftermath of Pearl Harbor. Yet by the late twentieth century, a new Asian migration was underway, spurred in part by the return of Hong Kong to China in 1997. As a result, today's B.C. and more especially the Lower Mainland, has an increasingly Asian component to its population and a high level of intermarriage across the old racial divides. Many in the city and the province, moreover, see their future as closely linked to the emergence of the Asia-Pacific sphere as the core of the twenty-first-century global economy. Under such a scenario, B.C. would be anything but an island onto itself.

What might emerge out of the conjuncture of the four templates I have just outlined? As the physicist Niels Bohr once quipped, "Prediction is very difficult, especially about the future." So let me offer a parting thought instead. We are still waiting for the Caucasian, the Asian, and the Indigenous; the cosmopolitan, the regional, and the national; the economic drive for more and the ecological need for less to find an appropriate balance. If and when they do, B.C. will have found its way.

CHAPTER 10

Explorations, or The Leisure of the Theory Class

IN THE COURSE OF my academic career, I have had the opportunity to travel extensively while attending conferences and workshops overseas or as a visiting professor at a number of universities. *The New York Times* once ran an opinion piece, reversing the title of Thorstein Veblen's famous book, *The Theory of the Leisure Class*, to read *The Leisure of the Theory Class*. Tongue in cheek, I thought it a fitting subtitle for this section.

My purpose here, expanding on journal entries that I have written over the years, is to record how exposure to far-ranging parts of the world has widened my horizons and permitted further reflection on political and other themes. To evoke the metaphor with which I began this memoir, the river of my childhood came to mingle with many other rivers to become my home *imaginaire*.

AUG. 1979, MOSCOW: The Congress of the International Political Science Association, a triennial affair at the time, was held in the Soviet Union. There was considerable controversy about the choice of venue — the Cold War was still raging — and some of this inevitably percolated into the sessions. Still, there were possibilities for some of the Western delegates, myself included, to meet with figures like Andrei Sakharov and younger dissidents as well as with more free-thinking students or academics so as to form our own impressions of what was still a fairly closed society.

To cut to the quick, party control one understood was omnipresent, especially in appointments to the higher levels of all major institutions. There were perks and privileges accruing to the *nomenklatura*, not available to ordinary Soviet citizens. "The collective prince 'i.e. party' that rules the land gives to its leaders five, nay ten times the measure, it gives to others. Not so very different from the distribution of wealth in our own capitalist paradise," I noted in my journal. Absenteeism, I heard one evening from a young Soviet researcher I had befriended, was a serious problem in the workplace; divorce rates among young couples were extremely high; and the craving for consumer goods, e.g. private automobiles, could not be met. Drunkenness was also a clearly visible problem when one ventured into a restaurant in downtown Moscow on an evening outing.

A revealing moment for me came when I visited a museum in the Kremlin containing treasures accumulated by the Czars. The gold and silver plate, the crowns and jewels, were evidence of an oppressive state power which had long preceded the Bolsheviks. What particularly struck my eye was a carriage, a gift from an English monarch of the sixteenth century (Elizabeth I?) to a Russian Tsar (Ivan IV, the Terrible?). This carriage had no steering wheel, so when it came to a crossroads its occupants would have to disembark, as the serfs lifted it and shifted it 90 degrees. To me this was a metaphor for Mother

Russia. 1917 comes along, all must disembark, the carriage of state is shifted 90 degrees, still without a steering wheel permitting any real flexibility as it plunges along.

As I write this today, I wonder whether things have changed that dramatically with Vladimir Putin in charge. There is a sad record of autocracy in Russia that had already been noted by Astolphe de Custine, a French visitor to that country in the 1830s during the reign of Nicholas I.

In his *Letters from Russia*, Custine had noted, before embarking on the ship in northern Germany that would carry him to St. Petersburg, the happy faces of the Russians who had just disembarked and the long faces of those about to return home. As an aristocrat, he had an opportunity for a private meeting with the Tsar. Nicholas I told him that he could speak freely in his presence. As Custine observed in his *Letters*: "The Tsar is the only person in Russia with whom one can speak freely."

Political cultures cannot be easily transformed. And though Mikhail Gorbachev, to give him his due, attempted to do just that, Russia has since reverted to the more top-down authoritarian style that has characterized so much of its history.

JULY 1991, BUENOS AIRES. INTERNATIONAL POLITICAL SCIENCE ASSOCIATION CONGRESS: This marked my first visit to the other America, after a long, but not impossibly fatiguing journey. Buenos Aires is a strange city, with its relatively modern airport and semi-modern autoroute leading from it, followed by the red-roofed tiles of its more prosperous suburbs, and then two shanty towns that could come straight out of the Third World. Concrete blocks and anonymous streets lead to the downtown core, with elements of grandeur — like the 9 de Julio Avenue. Harmony is somehow lacking, quite attractive buildings here and there slapped side by side with modern-day atrocities or nondescript office/apartment buildings of all types.

The young women are strikingly good-looking, with their thin cheeks and fine features. The students at the Congress seem more formal than their North American counterparts. And there is a melancholy about the place, a sense of sadness, if not of hopelessness, that may be cultural in character, or economic — Argentina has just been through one of its periodic currency crises.

The Congress itself is a reasonable mix of panels, many focusing on the democratization theme, both where Latin America and Central Europe are concerned. There are eminent panelists like Fernando Henrique Cardoso, a sociologist studying Latin American dependency and development and a future president of Brazil, and interesting insights to be gleaned about the influence that both European and North American paradigms in the social sciences have had on Latin America.

I visit some of the city's main sites: the old immigrant quarter, La Boca; the elegant San Martín Theatre with its evenings of tango, La Recoleta Cemetery with its ornate mausoleums reminiscent of Père Lachaise in Paris and with the flower-bedecked tomb of Evita; the fine arts museum; and the posh Santa Fe and Florida district. I reflect on the poetry and short stories of Borges — his *Aleph* in particular — and on the politics of the country. Too much of a military touch, with the statues to José de San Martín, Argentina's liberator, Juan Manuel de Rosas, Argentina's caudillo between 1829–1852, and similar figures. A populist tone, viz. the cult to Evita Perón I witness not only in the cemetery but in posters around town to mark the thirty-ninth anniversary of her death.

In many ways, the Peróns foreshadowed the form of populism that has appeared in countries as diverse as Venezuela, Hungary, Turkey, the Philippines, and the United States in our own day.

Democratic elections result in victory for a strong-armed candidate, who lambastes the traditional political establishment, while promising magic cures to the economic ills, the corruption, or the unrest sweeping a country.

Once in power, such leaders offer bromides of one sort or another to their followers, while clamping down hard on their opponents. Constitutional niceties are swept aside and due process, free speech, and the like treated as the currency of fools. There is a blatantly authoritarian touch to such regimes, though falling short of the more extreme forms of the one-man rule that Hitler, Stalin or Mao came to embody.

Still, there are lessons to be learned by those who take liberal democracy seriously. Elected parties have got to govern in the interests of all members of society, not of some narrow, elite group. They need to address the social needs of the lower 50 percent, the *descamisados* or shirtless ones, as they were known in Argentina. But they need to do so in a way that does not involve endless demagoguery and the conspiracy theories that accompany it.

There was a further lesson to be drawn from my week in Argentina. The most poignant moment of my stay was joining the Madres de la Plaza de Mayo marching in a nearby square and listening to two of the mothers who had come to the Political Science Congress to tell their tales of children never to be seen again, of grandchildren abducted into unknown hands. The valley of tears the country was put through during the years of military dictatorship between 1976–83 and the thousands of "disappeared" would not be easily forgotten. Nor would the scars quickly heal. We who have been spared military regimes can thank our lucky stars.

AUG. 1994, BERLIN: Another International Political Science Association Congress, and my first time back to this city since the fall of the Wall. My hotel is in the old East Berlin, and travelling the route by tram along the Lindauer Allee and then changing to the subway at the Rosa-Luxemburg-Platz to cross West Berlin to the convention centre where the Congress is being held is an experience in itself. It is as though the history of this until recently divided city and country were unfolding before my eyes. As for the Congress: there was a very useful series of panels and papers touching on the recent burgeoning of civil society in Central Europe and beyond.

My sharpest memory, however, is linked to a side trip I made to Weimar and Buchenwald, in the company of Caroline Andrew and Jeanne Laux, two colleagues from the University of Ottawa. Weimar, beautifully restored, the city of Goethe, Schiller, Herder, the Bauhaus, represented the flowering of what had been richest in the German cultural tradition. It was also famous for the 1919 constitution that was drafted here and the short-lived Weimar Republic which perished with the Nazi accession to power in 1933.

Buchenwald is a mere eight kilometres from Weimar. What a stark contrast between the latter's picturesque market square and cobbled streets and Buchenwald's grim barracks of 1937–45, the Karachoweg to the left of the railway tracks down which prisoners were herded like frightened cattle, the crematoria which awaited those who had been executed or driven to exhaustion through the merciless exactions of the S.S. *"Jedem das Seine"* — "to each his due" — is the sign which the Brownshirts erected at the entrance to the camp. What took place here inevitably tarnishes the beauty of Weimar and the surrounding Thuringian woods, reminding the visitor of the barbarism which the great literary culture of this country associated with Goethe or Schiller could not prevent.

Yet Germany, more convincingly than many other countries, has come to terms with the ghosts in its recent past. The Bundesrepublik of today is a model of liberal democracy, having broken radically with what the Nazi interlude spelled, and with an earlier more authoritarian tradition, the so-called *Sonderweg* or separate way, that had differentiated Germany from its Western neighbours. What this shows is that political cultures are not always impermeable to change and that countries, no less than individuals, can fruitfully learn from their past.

MAY 2003, BERLIN: I am back in Germany's capital city for four days, from Paris where I have been spending the year, to attend a conference of foreign policy wonks on Canada's role in the current American-Old Europe spat over the Iraq War. I get to deliver my "European Roots of Canadian Identity" argument without provoking a hostile reaction — quite the contrary.

I like Berlin as a city. It has an easier, less formal feel to it than Paris, with its inhabitants less in love with themselves or with the past. There is also a lot more by way of green spaces to give it a livable quality. Not that parts of the Mitte could not do with substantial repair. Or that the new malls and office towers by Potsdamer Platz don't have a North American feel to them.

I make a return visit to the Pergamon Museum. Once again, I am overwhelmed by the fidelity to the human form of the Greek and Roman sculptures, by the massive columned altar from Pergamon with its friezes. And the Assyrian antiquities and the soaring Gates of Babylon set my mind reeling in other directions.

If there is one thing that brings me close to an epiphany on this visit, it is a newly released film, *Good Bye, Lenin!* with its clever and poignant depiction of the fall of the German Democratic Republic (East Germany). It is the tale of a mother who was a true believer in the old regime and of her son who, following his mother's stroke and short-lived coma at the moment of the Fall, maintains her in her faith for the remaining year of her life. We are children of the world in which we were reared and of the beliefs which were instilled in us. We are also capable of great fidelity, like Alexander to his mother, a fidelity that takes on a life of its own giving a purpose to our existence when political belief systems seem to have collapsed.

And collapse they do, as was certainly true of the Soviet-style communist system after 1989. At one level, not something to be regretted. Still, as my conversation last night with Thomas Greven, a German colleague, underlines, the left at the moment has lost any convincing alternative to the capitalist/market model. Trade unions everywhere are on the defensive, and one wonders whether the worm will ever turn again. So goodbye Lenin, and back to the stark reality of Islamist attacks in Casablanca, venture capitalists on the make, and SARS threatening to unleash one of the horsemen of the Apocalypse onto the planet.

OCT. 23–30, 1998, CADIZ: A Canadian Studies conference. I stare at the waters from which the ships of Isabella the Catholic and her successors set out to conquer the New World. In the museum: Phoenician vases, Roman funerary objects, paintings of the Madonna and saints. There are porous rocks along the cobbled inner-city streets, tiles and stained wood, and squares with lofty palms and baobabs. Morocco is a stone's throw away, as the Pillars of Hercules stand guard over the Mediterranean.

Once the conference ends, I leave with Paco Colom, a colleague from Madrid, as my guide. Cordoba, with its many-pillared mosque and haunting echoes of the Sephardim in its Barrio Judío, the world of Maimonides and of the poet, Yehuda Halevi. The Archivo General de Indias in Seville with its untold number of documents of the New World. Madrid with its Residencia where I lodge for several nights, a residence that bears the imprint of Lorca, Dali, and Buñuel who were students together here in the early 1920s. The treasures of the Prado, with its exhibit on the world of Philip II. Barcelona, where I give a talk on the dialectic played out between majority and minority nationalities, and fall in love once again with its wide avenues and surreal architecture.

For the moment, the national question in Spain seems to be in abeyance. But Catalonia follows its own drummer. The Catalan language, as old and venerable as Spanish, has been revived now that the Franco dictatorship has bitten the dust. A visit to the Museum of Catalan History down near the harbour dispels any illusion that Catalans and other Spaniards view their history in one and the same way. It will come as no surprise to me when barely a decade later a strong secessionist movement would make its appearance in the region.

JUNE 2000, SANTIAGO: The pilgrimage city of Santiago de Compostela, one of the European Union's cultural capitals this year, where I am attending a workshop on nationalism. In the alcove of my newly refurbished hotel room — as enticing a room as it has been my good fortune to inhabit in many a year — I look out at a green meadow and the stone walls of one of the innumerable religious buildings that mark this town.

Am I moved by the religious imagery in the cathedral which I visit this afternoon? Not really — it is too far from my own lived experience, too heavily inculcated with the rituals of a medieval Church more known for its persecuting zeal than for its tolerance. Nor can I take to heart legends of the apostle James's bones being miraculously transported here. These have everything to do with the need for Catholic counter-myths to Islam at the dawn of the Reconquista. The words *Santiago matamoros* (St. James, the slayer of Moors) are engraved on the facade of the cathedral, lest one not get the message.

At the same time, there is something faintly moving about
groups of young people and their elders arriving with their staffs to
make the final ascent into the old town. Many of those walking the
Camino today are not doing so out of some orthodox faith, but in
search of something vaguely spiritual in an increasingly secular and
materialistic age. There is a seven-hundred-year link to the past
associated with the Camino, much like the more than five hundred
years since the foundation of the University of Santiago, where my
workshop is being held.

The workshop itself is a pleasant experience. A chance to renew
friendships with the Canadians/Québécois present — Guy Laforest, Alain Gagnon, Will Kymlicka, Wayne Norman. To meet Fer-
ran Requejo from Barcelona, Bhikhu Parekh and John Loughlin
from the U.K., as well as local participants like Ramón Máiz. To
present my views on the interplay between recognition and *ressentiment* in the internal dynamics of multinational states. I argue that
the bottom line for the majority population in multinational states,
for example English Canadians in the Canadian case, is the desire
to retain common citizenship and an ongoing state structure with
Québécois, coupled with *ressentiment* towards hard-line Quebec
separatists who would undermine this. For members of minority
nationalities like the Québécois, the bottom line is the desire for
recognition of their distinct national identity, coupled with *ressentiment* towards those English Canadians who would deny this. To
the degree that federal-type arrangements with asymmetrical features can simultaneously address these two bottom lines, multinational states like Canada can endure.

JUNE 24, 2000, GALICIA. LA FÊTE DE LA SAINT-JEAN: Spent in
the company of Guy Laforest and his sister Judith on a car trip to
the coast of Galicia. The coast is dotted with picturesque coves,

and the vegetation along the byways where we walk brings us face to face with mountain flowers in shades of pink and yellow, while just below us, is the sea with its hump-backed waves.

The high point of the excursion is Cape Finisterre, an impressive promontory at the westernmost point of Spain looking straight out to the Atlantic. More than Santiago with its Old World religiosity, this is where one should come to meditate upon the human condition, on the boundary between sea and land, on the power of the wind and of the waves, sweeping all before them. The Coast of Death they called it in Gallego (the language of Galicia), and one need but imagine the number of fishing and other vessels to have gone down off these shores.

As a species originating in the sea, we experience a powerful sensation at such moments, as though we have come back to the womb. The sound of the waves both evoke and strangely calm our primordial fears. So ancient humans must have gazed out from land's end. So too Spanish sailors, setting off in their galleons for the New World five centuries ago. As for twenty-first-century humans, for all our technological gimmickry, one cannot help feeling a sense of awe in its presence.

AUTUMN 1999, CANBERRA: Mahie and I have crossed the equator to an island continent that for three months we will call home. A British/European/multicultural offshoot in the South Pacific. A language, for all its accented differences, that one can easily understand, a sense of physical space, even sprawl, that evokes our northern home. Fauna and flora to beguile visitors from afar.

I am here as a Visiting Fellow in the Research School of the Australian National University. Pleasant company in the political science department, Brian Hindess especially, morning and afternoon teas to chat with colleagues, the National Gallery with its

Australian equivalents to our Group of Seven, the National Library, the War Museum with its evocation of Gallipoli on the one hand, Japanese prison camps on the other. A modernistic Parliament building when compared to ours, but a strangely planned city, Canberra, with no real centre to it, unlike Ottawa.

I get down to the task of researching and writing, making good use of the stacks in the Chifley and Menzies libraries. On the whole a productive semester. And plunk in the middle of our stay the referendum on whether to scrap the British monarch as Australia's head of state to be replaced by an appointed president.

NOV. 6, 1999, CANBERRA: Referendum day in Australia. The "Yes" side to becoming a republic seems headed for defeat, for much the same reason that Charlottetown went down back home in 1992 — a mistrust of politicians. "Say No to the Politicians' Republic" has proven a diabolically successful slogan, allowing both conservative defenders of the monarchy and advocates of direct election of a president to join forces in voting down the proposed model. The kind of compromises which proved necessary on the republican side to win cross-party and elite support proved lethal when it came to securing popular approval.

The underlying story of this campaign is not only republicanism vs. monarchy but also republicanism vs. democracy. Republicanism can translate very simply into non-monarchical forms of rule. In addition, there is in the spirit of republicanism, both ancient Roman and modern, a mistrust of unalloyed popular sovereignty. The Australian elites — the so-called Chardonnay republicans of Sydney and Melbourne — were perfectly content with an appointed president, the better to turn the page on monarchical symbolism that had had its day. But many in Australia, while not enamoured of monarchical trappings, were strongly mistrustful of a scheme that failed to give *them* the final say in choosing the head of state through an elected president.

Overall, it has been a fairly low-keyed debate, with relatively little evidence of popular interest. For an issue that touches directly on the question of national identity — What is Australia on the eve of the twenty-first century? Who are Australians? — it has failed to strike real fire among large sections of the population. I can contrast that with the role that nationalism has played in places like Catalonia, the Basque Country, Flanders, Scotland, Quebec. Is it the case that the nationalist *imaginaire* has a more jaded quality in mainstream liberal democracies at the end of the twentieth century? Or that political passions do not run all that deeply in our hyper-individualistic age?

I regret, as a Canadian with strongly republican sympathies of my own, that this referendum has failed. For it is surely an anomaly that in the twenty-first century, both Australia and Canada will have as their head of state a foreign monarch. I do not bear any antipathy to constitutional monarchies per se — Scandinavia, the Netherlands, Belgium, the United Kingdom, Spain or Japan today, are examples of where it works perfectly well. But Elizabeth II and her heirs will never be Australian or Canadian citizens. And how can a people be truly sovereign if their formal head of state is not a citizen of their own country? Had Australia voted in favour of a republic, I am quite convinced that Canada would have eventually followed suit. A missed opportunity for both of our countries that will not soon return.

JAPAN (ON THREE SEPARATE OCCASIONS, 1997, 1998, 1999): Three days in Tokyo. A sprawling city of skyscrapers and department stores, expressways and subway lines befitting a leading metropolis of the global economy. Andrew Dewit, a former PhD student of mine, has been pleasant company, accompanying me on my visits to the War Museum which has stirred much controversy over the years and to the National Museum with its extensive collection of Japanese prints and ceramics.

I feel surprisingly at home in Japan. Its pattern of life has been conveyed to me through film, art, sushi, as well as the political or historical writings that I have read. This is one of the two Asian societies — India being the other — that have fascinated me since my adolescent years.

In Kyoto for the next three days. An opportunity to meet faculty at Ritsumeikan University, with which UBC has entered into an agreement for student and faculty exchanges. I hit it off particularly well with Yoshi Nakatani, a political scientist of left-wing views. He will translate my newly published book, *Twenty-First Century Democracy*, into Japanese, and this will lead to invitations both in 1998 and 1999 to return and give a series of guest lectures on the subject. On those two occasions, Mahie will accompany me and strike up a warm friendship with his wife, Michiko.

There is a serenity to the temples and shrines of Kyoto that I will always cherish. So too to the surrounding hills and landscape and to the adjacent bamboo forest. The city has a human scale, more so than Tokyo, and there is an ambient politeness to human interactions, e.g. rituals of greeting, quite unlike what one is accustomed to in North America. At the same time, Japan is a country that has been able to combine advanced technology with an aesthetic steeped in deep cultural traditions, and this cannot fail to fascinate the Western visitor. The community dimension — in the broadest sense of the term — matters, and people for the most part are not simply encouraged to do their own thing.

This lack of individualism can be a problem, I will discover, when delivering my lectures in 1998 and 1999, for it is rather hard to get Japanese students to speak up in class or to ask questions. Nor does Japan, as its modern history would suggest, have the same deep-rooted democratic traditions that we find in Western Europe or North America. The Meiji Restoration of 1868, in building a resiliently modern Japanese state, also gave rise to the militarism that culminated in the invasion of Manchuria and China in the 1930s and the unprovoked aggression of World War II. As for the post-war years, the same political party, the Liberal Democrats, has been in power for almost the entire time.

In other respects, however, Japan has lessons to impart. Perhaps the most striking for me were some of the Buddhist precepts I discovered during my stays there. A few of these I jotted down, and they strike me as wisdom of the highest order:

- "Hatreds never cease by hatred in this world. By love alone they cease. This is an ancient law."
- "Though he should conquer a thousand men in the battlefield a thousand times, yet he, indeed, who would conquer himself is the noblest victor."
- "People love their egoistical comfort, which is a love of fame and praise. But fame and praise are like incense that consumes itself and soon disappears."

JULY 2006, FUKUOKA, JAPAN: An International Political Science Association Congress, the last I will attend. There is nothing particularly beautiful about this city with its wide avenues and modern office buildings. There is less exoticism to my visit to Japan this time, since I had had my initial immersion in "Japanism" in the 1990s. The only appealing view I have seen to this point is the one from the convention centre onto Hakata Bay, ringed by mountains with ferries and other craft making the crossing from the southern island of Kyushu on which Fukuoka is located to the main Japanese island of Honshu, 10 to 12 kilometres away.

I feel stimulated by some of the sessions I attend, on language and politics, on democratic theory. But there is a melancholy side to this visit, knowing that I have had to come here by myself, now that Mahie has had her stroke. This sense of melancholy is reinforced by my brief interaction at the Congress with Katsu, a warm-hearted graduate student whom Mahie and I had befriended in Kyoto on our visits there; by lunch with Yoshi Nakatani and the coffee-table book about Kyoto that he offers as a gift from Michiko and him to Mahie and me — a reminder of the time when the two of us could journey to that most beautiful of Japanese cities. *Sayonara*, I am tempted to write, to a Japan we once experienced as a couple, poetic, illuminating, and now irretrievably fading away.

• • •

The travel which I have been describing in this section provided me with a feel for the diversity of polities that constitute our planet. It made me a political scientist with a firmer grasp of the comparative dimension of my discipline and for the need to take varying historical experiences and institutional traditions seriously. It allowed me to develop friendships with colleagues across national lines and to bring some of their insights to bear in my own academic work. In a world where the Internet and Facebook have come to dominate so much of our fellow citizens' time, two cheers for the face-to-face contact and cultural richness that direct exposure to other societies can provide.

CHAPTER 11

On the Passage of Time

AS WE AGE, we become ever more conscious of time. I can still recall as a child of eleven back in 1955, thinking to myself how very distant the year 2000 seemed to be. And so it was. But the decades have come and gone, loved ones and friends have died, the twentieth century is past history and the first two decades of the twenty-first have quickly pealed away.

I turned seventy-five in 2019. Far more of my life lies behind me than still lies ahead. Inevitably the past I have known comes to loom ever larger, even as the future is something I will never know. In this penultimate section, I offer some reflections, both general and more personal, on the passage of time.

The great French historian of feudalism, Marc Bloch, who perished fighting in the French Resistance, cites an Arab proverb: "People resemble their own epoch more than they resemble their fathers." How very true. Each generation is burdened with its own lived experience, quite different from the experience of the one that preceded or will follow. It is not surprising that one takes comfort in the company of friends with whom one went to school, roomed together at some crucial moment in one's life, shared music or sporting events, lived through some seminal collective experience — economic breakdown or long periods of prosperity, war, dictatorship, liberation, major social transformation, and so on. We are children of our age and this can be more important in forging identities than any other characteristic.

I realize, in my own case, just how much I was a child of the 1960s. I came of age in a period when old verities were being cast aside. Quebec was shedding both its traditional Catholic beliefs and the paternalistic style of politics that had dominated the province. The Third World, as it came to be called, had been affirming its independence from its long-time colonial rulers. The Berlin Wall had been built in 1961 and the Cuban Missile Crisis of 1962 had brought the United States and the Soviet Union to the brink of nuclear war. Yet détente would come in its aftermath and, in the longer run, an end to the Cold War. The Civil Rights movement would bring a new impulse to race relations in the United States, and the anti-war movement help precipitate the eventual American withdrawal from Vietnam.

There was a hopefulness in the air, as the Baby Boomer generation sought to do things differently from its elders. Some might turn to drugs; others to communal living; still others return to the land. New social movements were emerging, as angry protests swept colleges and universities throughout the developed world from Japan to Western Europe to North America.

Post-war prosperity had brought close to full employment in its wake, and governments were in an expansionary mood, embarking on new social programs. Members of the '60s generation would be among its major beneficiaries, constituting the largest university-educated cohort to date, and having little reason to worry about their long-term career prospects. Theirs was an enviable situation, quite unlike what the Depression generation had experienced or, for that matter, the millennials who were to follow.

Once the cultural effervescence and political upheaval of the 1960s had subsided, a sober aftermath ensued. The hopes that many in the '60s might have entertained of ushering in a more just and egalitarian world would prove short-lived. There were breakthroughs on issues like censorship, gender equality, or sexual orientation. But powerful elites continued to dominate the commanding heights of the economy — an increasingly globalized economy as the decades wore on. High levels of unemployment would return, as deindustrialization became the scourge of long-established manufacturing centres unable to hold their own against cheaper foreign competition. Political institutions, for all the talk about participatory democracy that had transpired, would retain their top-down character. Members of the '60s generation would learn what generations before theirs had also learned — that they could not, through pure determination, remake the world entirely in their own image.

Generational cohorts are not the only ones to experience the vagaries of fortune; the same is true for countries and regimes. Rise and fall has been a persistent theme through recorded history, ancient no less than modern, Eastern no less than Western. The period since World War II would prove no exception.

One salient example would be the eclipse of the European empires which from the fifteenth century on had held sway over large portions of the globe. The United Nations which had 51 member states in 1945, the year of its creation, now has 193, most of these ex-colonial states. The United Kingdom and France may retain permanent seats on the Security Council; by no stretch of the imagination are they still the great powers they once were. The European Union, for its part, may occupy an important place in the economic scheme of things. But its political clout is far weaker and there is little reason to believe, given the continued importance of national sovereignty, that its role in this regard will increase any time soon.

Another dramatic example of rise and fall would be the disintegration of the Soviet Union and of the East European bloc which it had once controlled. The Russian Revolution had been a seminal event of the early twentieth century, mobilizing support from millions around the world. The Soviet feat of arms in World War II, achieved at a horrific cost in human lives, had seemed to cement the country's place as one of the world's two great powers. Within forty-five years all had come to naught. And with it the dream of burying capitalism and of constructing a communist world order in its place.

Japan, despite its crushing defeat in World War II, experienced dizzying rates of growth from the 1950s on. So much so, that some predicted its eventual displacement of the United States as the leading capitalist power. Yet by the 1990s, the country was becoming the prototype of economic stagnation and demographic decline. This downward spiral was as dramatic as the upward curve that Japan's immediate neighbour, China, was to experience.

No one looking at the wreckage that had constituted the Great Leap Forward of the late 1950s or the Cultural Revolution of the mid-1960s, could have predicted where China would find itself five decades later. Yet in the aftermath of the reforms inaugurated by Deng Xiaoping from the late 1970s on, new industries, cities, and transportation grids have been springing up like mushrooms, hundreds of millions have been lifted out of abject poverty, and China is becoming a great power again, increasingly in competition with the United States.

As for the United States, it was indisputably in command of the non-communist world after 1945, and seemingly the sole remaining hegemonic power after the break-up of the Soviet Union. Yet its hegemony seems less certain, as the twenty-first century unfolds. The alliance system carefully constructed during the Cold War years is fraying badly, in part, but only in part, because of the "America First" impulses of the current occupant of the White House. At the same time, the liberal democratic order which the United States once claimed to champion is being challenged once again by authoritarian regimes. "The American century," which Henry Luce and *Life Magazine* had celebrated in 1941 may be becoming a thing of the past, as the world's population careens towards 10 billion and beyond, as non-Western states come into their own, and as climate change threatens to wreak havoc with the future of the planet, including coastal areas of the United States itself. Previous empires, from the Carthaginian to the Roman, from the Spanish to the British, have bitten the dust. So, in due course, will the American. History does not play favourites.

Memory, however, does. So let me turn to memories of things that have marked me over the years.

I'll begin with cinema, something I have much savoured since my adolescence. Two examples from that early period come to mind. The first was a Russian production of *Boris Godunov*, an opera I knew nothing about, but which quickly held me in its sway. The chorus, the scenes with falling snow, the pealing bells, the deep baritone voices evoked a mysterious world, helping to instill a strong interest in Russian history and things Russian that would remain with me for many years. The second example was Satyajit

Ray's magisterial *Pather Panchali*. Set in a Bengali village in the latter years of the Raj, its depiction of extreme poverty was an eye-opener. At the same time, the tenderness of family relations shone through as did the pathos of the mother's death, something I have never forgotten. In visiting India as an academic many years later, I found myself reliving something of the magic of that first celluloid encounter with the sub-continent.

Two other films also affected me strongly. One was *Hitler: A Film from Germany* by Hans-Jürgen Syberberg, which I saw in the early 1980s. Puppets played a memorable part, mad King Ludwig II of Bavaria gesticulating wildly, anticipating the greater madness yet to come; Richard Wagner and his *Ring Cycle*; Horst Wessel with a list of Nazi stalwarts; and Adolf ranting much as in his speeches of yesteryear. There were also live actors, notably a young man asking the questions Why? Wherefore? Can any of us be innocent?

I asked myself then what it meant to revisit such material, to remind my generation of fascism's extraordinary appeal a mere half-century before. And here we are again, forced to ask ourselves: "Can fascism return?" The answer is probably "No," at least not in identical fashion to what the 1920s and 1930s experienced. But the cult of the leader, the demonization of minorities, a diminished faith in liberal democratic values have not proven to be in short supply in troubled times.

Another film I still vividly remember is the Japanese trilogy by Masaki Kobayashi, *The Human Condition*. Its central character, a Japanese soldier named Kaji, serving in Manchuria during the Japanese-Chinese war, is an epic human being, not born that way, but coming to live out a destiny that culminates in his death in the Siberian waste. Kaji is the receptacle chosen to play out an unsung part, the good Japanese caught up in the military machine with all its crimes, yet able in some small ways to show his humanity, for example as a labour supervisor assigned to a workforce of Chinese prisoners. To be a hero on the victorious side brings its own reward, to be the victim as the Chinese are in this war still means to be on the side destined to triumph. But to uphold a code of good and evil in the camp of the oppressors is to stand out in a way that very few can ever do. The passage of time does little to diminish the message.

As for personal memories, these can take different forms. I recall frequent media appearances both on the CBC and Radio-Canada back in the 1980s and 1990s, which gave me exposure to a much larger audience than was my wont. One can easily be swept up in the excitement of the moment. But it all proved to be terribly ephemeral, much like the election results on which I would comment or the constitutional debates which ultimately went nowhere.

In much the same way, I can look back with a critical eye at the weekly or bi-weekly *Le Devoir* columns I wrote between 1995 and 1997. Had they done any good? Had I made even a modest contribution to the dialogue that needs to be fostered between Canadians and Québécois? Or was I, much like the André Laurendeau I so admired, something of a dreamer in a country whose very structure challenges its cohesion?

Where conferences are concerned, two particularly stick in my mind. One was a week-long affair held in Cerisy, Normandy, in early June 1995, in honour of Charles Taylor. It had something of the life of a secular monastery to it or of Thomas Mann's *Magic Mountain*, minus the T.B., transposed to the last decade of the twentieth century. A comfortable old chateau, antique furniture, sloping floors, vistas onto the meadows outside. High quality participants from France, other European countries and Canada. A week as part of a shared community, superb meals eaten together, three to four stimulating sessions a day, walks and excursions in the environs. If this was what community was about, I thought to my-self, I would be ready to live it all the time.

The second, a Constitutional Affairs conference, transpired in Quebec City in January 2008. It had a retro feeling to it, with re-hashed arguments about asymmetrical federalism, debates about Senate reform, and a "cock fight" between Bernard Landry and Eddie Goldenberg over Trudeau and constitutional patriation. What I recall most of all about this conference in Quebec City is the cold penetrating my face and hands as I made my way along the Grande Allée into the old city or walked the pathways in the nearby park that the Plains of Abraham have become. It would have been difficult to put down roots in such a hostile climate. Yet 400 years later, the original French settlement had flourished and a country we call our own — federal, multinational and multiethnic — had come to occupy the northern tier of the continent. *Les voya-geurs* were an important part of the story — the French Canadians who developed the fur routes both south along the Mississippi and westwards into the far-off regions of the continent. It was this will-ingness to venture into *le grand large* that colours the French Cana-dian contribution to the history of North America and some of the continent's place names from Detroit to Baton Rouge, Leduc to Juneau reflect this. It was a reminder to me of why Quebec had loomed so large in my own reflections on Canadian identity, even if the West Coast would ultimately become my home.

Some books I read over the years also left deep impressions. A few examples will suffice. Christopher Hill's *Milton and the English Revolution* and Matthew Scrivener's *Radical Shelley* brought home hard truths about the poetic and the political and about the era in which each of us is fated to live. Milton lived the triumph and ul-timate defeat of one revolution and his greatest works reflect it. Shelley, after 1815, lived in a period of counter-revolution and his greatest works anticipate an egalitarian, liberty-fostering alternative. The indignation that moved Shelley after the Peterloo Massacre of 1819, the recollection of the Good Old Cause that was Milton's in Restoration England remain models for dark times.

Pablo Neruda's *The Heights of Macchu Picchu* never fails to inspire. Everything he touched turned into poetry. Not just any kind of poetry, but as linguistically rich and variegated as the landscapes, countries and women that he had loved.

In reading Antonio Muñoz Molina's novel, *In the Night of Time*, I was struck by the figure of the political exile. Whether it was the former Bauhaus architect, Rossman, reduced to penury in the Madrid of 1935 or the main character, Ignacio Abel, himself forced into exile in America by the Spanish Civil War, exile remains a bitter experience. This is something one can never feel in one's flesh, unless one has been through it oneself. In today's world, the exiles come to us from far and wide — not all political exiles, by any means. But how difficult to put oneself into the shoes of the other, when one is living with all the comforts of home in a first world country that knows neither war nor grinding poverty.

Montaigne has been a frequent source of comfort for me in trying moments. He managed to preserve his equanimity through thick and thin, to overcome the loss of his closest friend, Étienne de La Boétie, to understand the challenge of solitude, and beyond that, the inevitability of death. But as he noted in one of his aphorisms, "*La mort est bien le bout, non pourtant le but de la vie.*" ("Death comes at the end of life, but is not its goal.")

This leads me to evoke sadder memories, associated with those who have departed. I recall my father's 70th birthday in Montreal, some forty years ago. I felt the passage of time, when my Uncle Joe and Aunt Jessie arrived from the States — frail old people with white hair. Uncle Joe kept talking about a distant past — Russia, childhood — as though it were but yesterday, and it was clear that he was at death's portal. My father and mother had also aged significantly. My brother, my sister, myself, my cousins would have to take over from our elders and carry on the family flame as best we could.

Two decades later, in 1997, I had to confront the death of my mother. I recall sitting in the early hours in the bedroom of my parents' apartment in Montreal, mirrors covered, black-and-white marriage picture on the wall, reflecting on her death. Orphaned almost at birth, sole survivor along with her brother of the ravages that did in European Jewry, ill almost unto death in some of my childhood years, she had been the keeper of the hearth through the decades of my adolescence and early adulthood. I had once been her cherished little one. Half a century had now gone by and those memories would fade even as her own memory gave out in the dim shadow state that marked her final years. The way of all flesh.

Five years later it was my father's turn. Philosophical though I tried to be about his passing — he had had his share of limitations after all, who doesn't? — I was fully aware that he had been my one remaining parent and the last survivor of his generation. I recall going through photo albums with my siblings one final time before they were dispersed, packing a few mementos into my suitcase, scanning the familiar rooms which I had visited whenever I had passed through Montreal. It was the end of an era, of a presence, of a world that had begun for me fifty-seven years earlier.

Close friends also began to fall by the wayside. In early 2010, I learned of my sociology colleague, Pat Marchak, succumbing to lung cancer. Her ordeal had stretched over months, culminating on New Year's Day. We had been close over the years, a shared interest in political economy, the NDP connection, numerous conferences, the Political Science affair of the mid-1990s when, as Dean of Arts at the time, she had not bought in to the chilly climate hysteria. She was progressive, but with her feet on the ground, serious in her scholarship, outgoing as a person. Someone I had cared for and whose disappearance, like that of other friends, would leave a hole.

The greatest challenge of all would be the chronic illnesses my wife endured, culminating in her death in November 2016. Hers was a long and difficult descent into the abyss — stroke, kidney failure, mobility issues, and in the end a failing heart. There is something very personal about the death of a loved one. Multitudes perish every day, sometimes under horrific conditions — Aleppo, boats sinking in the Mediterranean, ISIS attacks on Christmas markets or on Sri Lanka churches and hotels — but these do not sting in quite the same way. We are hard-wired to care intensely for our own. The *Bhagavad Gita* speaks of "time's destroying flames," from whose extended jaws "no shelter is to be found." Yet in an odd sort of way, the passage of time can to a small degree assuage the pain of dealing with the death of those whom one has loved.

A few other memories, some political, others more philosophical, are worth recording.

As I found my views evolving in the 1980s and 1990s, I felt myself no longer quite at home in the radicalism of my past but even less so in the material abundance and endless pursuit of wealth that has come to characterize our global capitalist age. Somewhere, I felt, there must be a better mix between things of the mind and of the body, between the living standards of some and the abysmal impossibility of living of others. Yet the realist in me knew all too well that this somewhere was not to be realized in the immediate here and now.

The twentieth century had given us Auschwitz, Hiroshima, and the Gulag, civil wars and regional conflicts, each often bloodier than the next. Technology had proven the great liberator from human drudgery on one hand, but the great polluter and destroyer of the earth on the other. Material abundance was a double-edged phenomenon, satiating our basic bodily needs, at least in the developed world, yet leaving so much else in our lives beyond reach.

As the old millennium was drawing to a close, I found myself thinking of Malthus, that late eighteenth-century prophet of gloom and doom, and his *Essay on the Principle of Population*. Could it be that he had been a true visionary after all, having seen the physical limitations to our species' endless multiplication and having integrated plague and famine into his analysis?

September 11, 2001, brought its own reflections. It seemed as though the twenty-first century had begun that day, with the attacks on the twin towers in Manhattan. At one level, I might have been tempted to see this as blow-back for what the United States, and the West more generally, had been perpetrating in the Arab world and beyond, shoring up one repressive regime after another. But for all the legitimate criticisms that could be aimed at American imperialism and its predatory behaviour, I knew that the world of jihadi extremism was profoundly inimical to my core values. There was no willingness on the part of its adherents to acknowledge the other, and more than anything else, that was the bottom line where the Enlightenment tradition to which I adhere was concerned. The world is not made whole through hatred, as the Buddhists for one acknowledge. Nor can terror succeed in ushering in a brave new world. It simply hardens the determination of those on the other side to resist its claims.

In early 2003, the drum beat for war in Iraq was getting louder and louder. Those in control of the White House and the Pentagon had decided to proceed; the opposition of world public opinion counted for little in comparison. The mind frame of the hawks, it seemed to me, was not very different from that of the Marxist-Leninists who had ruled the other half of a divided world until 15 to 20 years before — ideological certitudes, wooden language, the secret arcades of power, contempt for those who dared to differ.

A propos the passage of time, I recall an amusing anecdote from a BBC radio series of the 1920s focusing on famous exiles who had lived in London, cited in a 2009 re-broadcast. A long since retired employee of the British Museum who had known Marx had been interviewed for one of the programs: "'e made us work hard, fetching volumes. Nobody 'as 'eard of 'im since."

In 2010, I found myself briefly back in Madrid. Wandering through the Prado, I re-visited Bruegel's *Triumph of Death* for the third time, a painting that never fails to attract and mesmerize onlookers. The museum had finally been remodelled, allowing floor space for nineteenth-century Spanish paintings subsequent to Goya. One in particular drew my attention, dealing with the expulsion of the Jews in 1492 — Ferdinand and Isabella on their thrones, Jewish emissaries pleading for their community, and the Grand Inquisitor, Torquemada, angrily holding up a cross with its suffering Jesus. The picture spoke to the weight of centuries past and to religious intolerance of which we have not seen the last.

2011 witnessed dramatic events in the Arab world, the so-called Arab Spring. It was empowering to see tyrants swept away, fear suddenly changing camps, generations of young people coming to the fore in places like Tahrir Square, looking for something other than autocracy on the one hand, harsh Islamic precepts on the other. But what seemed a potential turning point for the Arab world rapidly fizzled out. Would things take a different turn in the future when popular uprisings would lead to the overthrow of the zombie ruler of Algeria and of the long-time dictator of the Sudan? Or would the Arab world continue to see authoritarian rulers with the army in control behind the scenes?

The 2014 Quebec provincial election inspired rather different thoughts. With the Parti Québécois reduced to 25 percent of the vote and 20 seats — an even poorer showing was to follow in 2018 — I could not help wondering if the outcome spelled the TKO for the Quebec sovereignty movement, the third No after the referendum defeats of 1980 and 1995?

The passion of an earlier generation seemed to have been spent, no longer resonating with a majority of the francophone population. Having flirted with sovereignty-association and sovereignty-partnership, that population had now decided to bury the question. There were more concrete priorities than *les lendemains qui chantent*.

What had begun with the Quiet Revolution and a generation dreaming of remaking the world anew had given way to a more sober reality. Long established states cannot be so easily broken up and the romantic aspiration of one generation gets ground down by the pragmatism of the next. *La guerre est finie* — at least it appeared to be so for the moment.

I could go on evoking memories from the past. For in looking back, as I have been doing in this section, I realize that there is consolation of a sort in invoking your family, your circle of friends, the things that mattered to your generation, the events that marked you, the bits of wisdom and illumination which came your way.

Towards the end of his multi-volume *Remembrance of Things Past*, Marcel Proust observed: "I realized that the writer does not need to invent the essential book, the only real book that matters, since it already exists inside each one of us. . . . The duty and task of the writer is that of a translator." In writing this memoir, I too have been a mere translator of thoughts and impressions that I've been carrying locked away for many years.

CHAPTER 12

What Was It All About?

AS I COME TO the end of my odyssey, I am tempted to ask the question, "What was it all about?" A question not unusual for people my age, looking back at the life they have led. But memory can play tricks, and the author of an account like this is not necessarily the same person as the younger one he sometimes evokes. The Portuguese poet, Fernando Pessoa, captured this well in one of his poems: "That who I am and that who I was / are two contrasting dreams."

Rather than aiming for the impossible, for pulling together disparate strands of a life into a single coherent whole, let me propose a different course. I'll evoke passages I have gleaned over the years from a wide range of sources and, in commenting on them, attempt to answer the question, "What was it all about?"

In *The Tale of Genji*, arguably the world's oldest extant novel, one reads the following: "The young are naked and the aged are cold." At one level this is simply about sexual drive and its eventual exhaustion. But at another level, it may imply that the young do not yet know the ways of the world and are relatively innocent in that regard. The aged, on the other hand, may know it all too well and have grown cold and cynical in the process. A warning that those of us over seventy need to heed.

Norberto Bobbio was an Italian political theorist who had cut his teeth in the underground opposition to Mussolini during World War II. In the memoir he wrote shortly before his death at ninety-four, he observed: "When you grow old, emotional attachments become more important than ideas." Here was a man whose life had been consecrated to the study of ideas — vital ones like liberty, equality, democracy, the left and the right. Yet he recognized that, as human beings, our emotional ties ultimately count for at least as much as ideas, that the friendships we forge and the love(s) we may have known weigh ever more heavily in the balance, especially towards the end of our lives. To which I can only say "Amen."

Another Italian, Giacomo Leopardi, arguably the greatest poet that country has produced since Dante, wrote the following:

My heart is shaken at the thought
Of how everything in the world goes by
And leaves so little trace.

Leopardi had a tragic sense of life, in part no doubt because he suffered from a terrible physical disability and died quite young. But those of us who stop to ponder for a moment what little will remain from the things that have kept us and our friends and colleagues so busily engaged know that Leopardi spoke a bitter truth.

As may have been true for Georg Trakl, an Austrian poet who also died young, in his case during World War I: "Only to him who despises happiness, comes knowledge." Something the ancient tragedians would have understood, but too easily forgotten today.

Perhaps we need to forget, in order to live our lives as fully as we can. As J.M. Coetzee observed in his novel *The Master of Petersburg*, "If we do not forget, they say, the world will soon be nothing but a huge library." Touché, I am tempted to admit, as someone who has spent many hours of his life in libraries and can now recognize the limits of all that accumulated knowledge. Yet with the destruction of the Library in Alexandria, much of what the ancients might have bequeathed us disappeared. More recently, the destruction wrought by ISIS in Palmyra or by its counterparts in Timbuktu left many in shock. We need to forget certain things in order to clear the cobwebs from our heads, but there is much from the past that needs to be remembered. After all, why undertake the writing of a manuscript like this, if there were no point remembering important moments in one's life?

An Egyptian scribe from the second millennium B.C. named Khakheperreseneb was perhaps the first to lament: "For what is said is merely repetition / and nothing is said that has not been said." This may sound outrageous to our ears, we who know the new discoveries that have been made by scientists through the ages, the inventions that have followed, the political and social transformations that modernity has wrought. But when it comes to human nature how much has really changed? And can we be certain that each generation, including our own, has not simply rediscovered old truths disguised as new?

"If you follow that which is within, you shall be free; if you do not, you shall be destroyed," reads a Gospel attributed to St. Thomas, dating from the second century AD in Egypt. If this passage appeals to me, it is because of a similar thought which I recorded in 1978: "I value my intellectual freedom over everything. This, no doubt, is why I make a bad Jew, a bad nationalist, and a bad Marxist. I insist on being my own person and will not bow meekly to any divinity or ideology."

In his memoir entitled *Itineraries*, whose title has inspired the title of this book, the Mexican poet and essayist, Octavio Paz, notes: "Much has been written about the post-war intellectual class's [left-wing] aberration, but it seems incomplete. Ripped out of the totality of ancient religious absolutes, we felt a nostalgia for totalities and absolutes." This captures something of the lure which ideologies can have, though it is by no means restricted to ideologies on the left like Marxism. There seems to be a human need for unchallengeable beliefs. Religion used to answer this, but in a more secular age, ideology can become a substitute. I can point to two instances of this in the Canadian context. In Quebec of the 1960s, intellectuals who had broken with the Catholicism of their youth — the group around the magazine *Parti pris* comes to mind — found in Marxism and doctrines of national liberation a worthy substitute. In English Canada of the late 1960s and 1970s, I was struck by the prominence of Jews like Peter Newman, Abe Rotstein, James Laxer, or Mel Hurtig in the new wave of nationalism that had emerged. Could the question of national identity have a peculiarly Jewish appeal? Were displaced Old Testament notions of national identity being resurrected, with the abandoned Jewish god of old now appearing as an agent of secular history?

The Israeli poet, Yehuda Amichai, once gave a reading at UBC. He made some comments about the different directions his life had taken and the political twists and turns he had experienced. Having exhausted the major ideologies of his day, he declared himself to be "a post-cynical humanist." I rather like that term. The word "humanist" by itself is vague, perhaps even pretentious. Cynicism, as I noted in my discussion of democracy, can be a particularly corrosive force. But having experienced it to some degree and having come out on the other side can be liberating in a way or at least restorative of one's faith in our highly imperfect species. And that species, as a sixteenth-century Japanese Zen Buddhist priest once remarked, despite differences in manner and speech, has the same nature everywhere. A useful reminder in an age like ours where national differences are over-emphasized and our shared humanity too easily swept aside.

The contemporary Japanese writer, Haruki Murakami, writes in one of his novels: "We have everything in this country. . . . The one thing we don't have is hope." This speaks to a broader theme of decline, culturally and intellectually, if not materially, very much in vogue in countries like Japan or France. The looming ecological crisis, moreover, engenders a sense of despair among many in the younger generation contemplating their future. I too find much to rue when I think of the self-destructive instincts of our species. But there is also the satisfaction which has come my way from watching the sun rise over Kyoto or Pelion, or feeling the *frissons* which great music or architecture or literary works provide, or from sharing in the delights of human company.

The Delphic oracle was known for her cryptic pronouncements. One of the most famous is contained in two simple words, "*Meden agan*," which translates as "Nothing in excess." This lends itself to different interpretations. For some this may be a call to respect the order of things, to never shake the boat, to learn to live within the limits one has been assigned. For others, contemplating today's world, this could be interpreted as a call to put limits on our material consumption, on our spoliation of the earth's resources, on the insatiable desire some have for wealth or power. I lean strongly towards the second interpretation, without entirely rejecting elements of the first. We need a balance in our lives and that, more than anything else, may be the answer to the question, "What was it all about?"

ABOUT THE AUTHOR

Philip Resnick was born in Montreal and pursued his university education at McGill, in Paris, and at the University of Toronto. For over forty years he was a member of the Department of Political Science at the University of British Columbia. His interests as a political scientist ranged widely, from Canadian politics and political economy to comparative nationalism and democratic theory. He has published ten highly regarded volumes on these topics. He is also a published poet, who began to write poetry in his adolescence and came to pursue this interest following his marriage to Andromache, who was Greek, over the many summers he and his family came to spend in Thessaly, in the city of Volos, and in a village and cove on adjacent Mount Pelion. He makes his home in Vancouver, British Columbia.